Edexcel GCSE
Religious Studies

Unit 16
Mark's Gospel

Hugh Thomas

ALWAYS LEARNING   PEARSON

Published by Pearson Education Limited, a company incorporated in England and Wales, having its registered office at Edinburgh Gate, Harlow, Essex CM20 2JE. Registered company number: 872828

www.pearsonschoolsandfecolleges.co.uk

Edexcel is a registered trademark of Edexcel Limited

Text © Pearson Education Limited 2009
First published 2009

13
10 9 8 7 6 5

British Library Cataloguing in Publication Data
A catalogue record for this book is available from the British Library

ISBN 978 1 846904 27 1

Edited by Florence Production Limited, Stoodleigh, Devon
Typeset by HL Studios, Long Hanborough, Oxford
Produced by Florence Production Limited, Stoodleigh, Devon
Original illustrations © Pearson Education Limited 2009
Illustrated by HL Studios, Long Hanborough, Oxford
Cover design by Pearson Education Limited
Picture research by Zooid
Cover photo/illustration © D. Hurst/Alamy
Printed in China (CTPSC/05)

Acknowledgements
The author and publisher would like to thank the following individuals and organisations for permission to reproduce copyright material:

Photos
akg-images, p24; p35; p42; p93; Alex Brandon/Associated Press/Press Association Images, p49; Boltin Picture Library/Bridgeman Art Library, p93; Cameraphoto/akg-images, p63; Ciurlionis State Art Museum, Kaunas, Lithuania/Bridgeman Art Library, p79; Clive Christian, p52; Colin Shepherd/Rex Features, p12; Coll. Archiv f.Kunst & Geschichte/akg-images, p48; Eddie Gerald/Alamy, p83; Electa/akg-images, p98; Electa/Museo dell'Opera Metropolitana/akg-images' p55; Electa/National Gallery of Ireland/akg-images, p71; Erich Lessing/akg-images, p41; p76; p110; Erich Lessing/Musee du Louvre/akg-images, p61; Eye Ubiquitous/Rex Features, p95; Franco Origlia/Getty Images, p20; Geoffrey Robinson/Rex Features, p44; Greg Balfour Evans/Alamy, p4; He Qi, p77; Hope Scotland, p7; Icon Distribution, Inc/Antonel/akg-images, p61; Isabella Stewart Gardner Museum, Boston, MA, USA/Bridgeman Art Library, p100; Jeff Morgan Religion/Alamy, p8; Jerry Bergman/Rex Features, p67; John Webb/National Gallery London/Art Archive, p32; Jupiterimages/Polka Dot /Alamy, p8; Karen Kasmauski/Science Faction/Corbis UK Ltd., p95; London Beth Din Kashrut Division, p37; Margo Harrison/Shutterstock, p87; Mike Blenkinsop/Alamy, p33; Ministero Beni e Att. Culturali/Photo Scala, Florence, p64; National Gallery, London/Superstock Ltd., p68; Neil Beer/Photodisc, p44; Nimatallah/Vatican Museums/akg-images, p112; P Deliss/Godong/Corbis UK Ltd., p85; Paula Solloway/Alamy, p11; Paula Solloway/Photofusion Picture Library, p21; Philipp Bernard/Photo RMN, p46; PhotoDisc, p86; Photolibrary Group, p14; p22; p65; Popperfoto/Getty Images p31; Rabatti Dominnie/Galleria d'Arte Moderna/akg-images, p74; René-Gabriel Ojéda/Photo RMN, p17; Robert Mulder/Still Pictures, p36; Russian State Museum/akg-images, p109; Sant'Apollinare Nuovo, Ravenna, Italy/Giraudon/Bridgeman Art Library, p71; Shangara Singh/Alamy, p73; Stefano Bianchetti/Corbis UK Ltd., p31; Superstock Ltd., p93; The Duke of Edinburgh's Award, p6; The Gallery Collection/Corbis UK Ltd., p104; The Photolibrary Wales/Alamy, p4; Thomas Cockrem/Alamy, p93; Tim Graham/Alamy, p10; White Images/Photo Scala, Florence, p78.

Text
Scripture taken from the Holy Bible, New International Version®. Copyright © 1973, 1978, 1984 International Bible Society. Used by permission of Zondervan. All rights reserved. p10 Quote: Permission granted by the Missionaries of Charity. p13 Statistics: With the permission of the Archbishops' Council, from the Anglican National Stewardship Committee 'Giving for life' ref. 951723. p16 Quote: Brainwave, the Irish Epilepsy Association, www.epilepsy.ie.

Every effort has been made to contact copyright holders of material reproduced in this book. Any omissions will be rectified in subsequent printings if notice is given to the publisher.

Websites
There are links to relevant websites in this book. In order to ensure that the links are up to date, that the links work, and that the sites are not inadvertently linked to sites that could be considered offensive, we have made the links available on the Heinemann website at www.pearsonschoolsandfecolleges.co.uk/hotlinks. When you access the site, the express code is 4271P.

Disclaimer
This material has been published on behalf of Edexcel and offers high-quality support for the delivery of Edexcel qualifications.

This does not mean that the material is essential to achieve any Edexcel qualification, nor does it mean that it is the only suitable material available to support any Edexcel qualification. Edexcel material will not be used verbatim in setting any Edexcel examination or assessment. Any resource lists produced by Edexcel shall include this and other appropriate resources.

Copies of official specifications for all Edexcel qualifications may be found on the Edexcel website: www.edexcel.com

Contents

Welcome to this Edexcel GCSE in Religious Studies Resource

These resources have been designed to build students' knowledge, understanding and skills, and to help prepare them for their GCSE Religious Studies assessment. Packed with exam tips and activities, these books include lots of engaging features to enthuse students and provide the range of support needed to make teaching and learning a success for all ability levels.

Features in this book

In each section you will find the following features:

- **an introductory spread** which introduces the topics and gives the Edexcel key terms and learning outcomes for the whole section

- **topic spreads** containing the following features:

  - **Learning outcomes** for the topic

  - edexcel ⋮⋮⋮ key terms

    Key terms are emboldened in the text and definitions can be found in the Glossary.

  - **Activities** and **For discussion** panels provide stimulating tasks for the classroom and homework

  - a topic **Summary** which captures the main learning points

  - passages from Mark's gospel are highlighted in blue for easy reference.

How to use this book

This book has been written to support you through your study of Edexcel GCSE Unit 16 Mark's Gospel.

The version of the Bible used is the New International edition.

A dedicated suite of revision resources. We've broken down the six stages of revision to ensure that you are prepared every step of the way.

How to get into the perfect 'zone' for your revision.

Tips and advice on how to plan your revision effectively.

Revision activities and exam-style practice at the end of every section plus additional exam practice at the end of the book.

Last-minute advice for just before the exam.

An overview of what you will have to do in the exam, plus a chance to see what a real exam paper will look like.

What do you do after your exam? This section contains information on how to get your results and answers to frequently asked questions on what to do next.

ResultsPlus

These features help you to understand how to improve your answers, with guidance on answering exam-style questions, as well as tips on how to remember important concepts and avoid common pitfalls.

There are three different types of ResultsPlus features throughout this book:

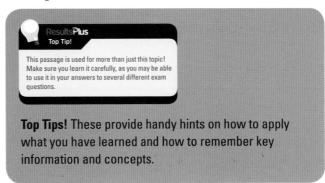

Top Tips! These provide handy hints on how to apply what you have learned and how to remember key information and concepts.

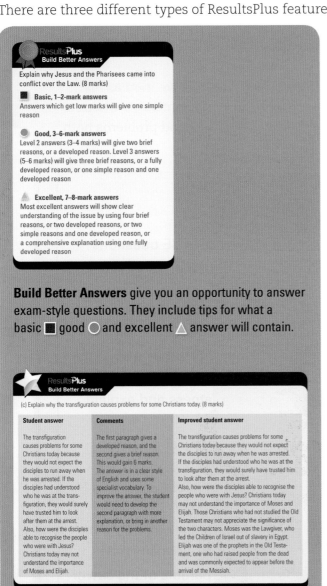

Build Better Answers give you an opportunity to answer exam-style questions. They include tips for what a basic ■ good ○ and excellent △ answer will contain.

The KnowZone **Build Better Answers** at the end of each section include an exam-style question with a student answer, comments on the answer and an improved answer so that you can see how to build a better response.

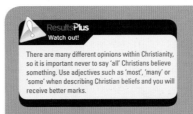

Watch out! These warn you about common mistakes and misconceptions that students often have.

Discipleship

Introduction

The purpose of this section is to help you investigate how Jesus chose twelve men as his closest followers and trained them to be disciples who would carry on his mission when he had left them. You will explore the meaning of discipleship and its costs and problems both then and to those who choose to follow Jesus today.

Learning outcomes for this section

By the end of this section you should be able to:

- give definitions of the key words and use them in answers to
- describe how the nature of discipleship is shown in the call and explain why it is important for Christians today
- describe how the nature of discipleship is shown in the send Twelve and explain how it affects ideas about Christians livi
- describe how the costs of discipleship are shown in Jesus' t explain how this teaching causes problems for some Christi
- describe how the costs of discipleship are shown in true gre why this teaching causes problems for some Christians toda
- describe how the costs of discipleship are shown in the rich why this teaching causes problems for some Christians toda
- describe how the costs of discipleship are shown in the para and explain what relationship this parable has to Christians
- describe how the problems of discipleship are shown in the boy and explain why this teaching causes problems for som
- describe how the problems of discipleship are shown in the and explain why Mark's account causes problems for Christi
- describe how the problems of discipleship are shown in Jes explain what this means for Christian living today
- describe how the problems of discipleship are shown in the disciples and explain how their failure might both help and Christians today
- describe how the problems of discipleship are shown in Pet explain how this might both help and cause problems for Cl
- express, with reasons, your own opinion on the topics cove and be able to explain the reasons why some people may d

edexcel ⋮⋮⋮ key terms

the commandments	the kingdom	self-sacrifice	true family
disciples	Levi	service	true greatness
the eye of a needle	Peter's denial	Sons of Zebedee	the Twelve

Jesus chose twelve men to be his special disciples. This may have been symbolic, as the Old Testament character Jacob, one of the Jewish patriarchs, had twelve sons. They in turn became the founders of the twelve tribes of Israel (Jacob himself had his name changed to Israel). By his choice of twelve men, Jesus may have been showing that he was sent by God for all the Jewish people.

Take a sheet of A3 paper, turn it landscape, and write 'Discipleship' in the middle of it.

- As a class, or in groups or pairs, make a list or chart outlining all the positive advantages that working on your own can bring.
- Next list the positive advantages of working as a member of a small group.
- Then list the disadvantages of both these ways of working.
- Finally, look at the three lists and use them to help you decide which is the best way of working.

Keep this in mind as we look at the theme of discipleship.

1.1 The call of the first disciples

Learning outcomes

By the end of this lesson, you should be able to:

● state the meaning of discipleship

● give your own opinion, with a reason, about the nature of discipleship as shown in the call of the first disciples

● explain why the nature of discipleship as shown in the call of the first disciples is important for Christians today.

edexcel ⠿ key terms

Disciples – Followers of Jesus.

Levi – A tax collector who was called to be a disciple.

Sons of Zebedee – The brothers James and John whom Jesus called to follow him.

Activities

1 You need to recruit four friends to join you in rebuilding a play area that has been vandalised

• Which four people would you choose?

• What qualities would you look for?

Explain why you have chosen these four.

Fishers of men

In the Jewish tradition, teachers of the law – rabbis – gathered people to learn from them in schools of **disciples**. Disciples would seek out and follow their rabbi, helping to spread their teachings.

As Jesus began his ministry he also recruited the first disciples to join him. In this passage from the gospel according to Mark, four fishermen give up their livelihood to follow Jesus:

'After John was put in prison, Jesus went into Galilee, proclaiming the good news of God. "The time has come," he said. "The kingdom of God is near. Repent and believe the good news!" As Jesus walked beside the Sea of Galilee, he saw Simon and his brother Andrew casting a net into the lake, for they were fishermen. "Come, follow me," Jesus said, "and I will make you fishers of men." At once they left their nets and followed him. When he had gone a little farther, he saw James **son of Zebedee** and his brother John in a boat, preparing their nets. Without delay he called them, and they left their father Zebedee in the boat with the hired men and followed him.'
(Mark 1:14–20)

The playground – before and after!

Activities

2 Who were the first four to follow Jesus?

3 What was their job before he took them away?

4 What were his words to them?

5 What do you think it was about Jesus that made them join him?

6 In groups of three, role-play an interview between a reporter and Simon and Andrew who are leaving town to work with Jesus.

Healthy people don't need doctors!

The next person whom Jesus calls to follow him is **Levi** – a tax collector. Tax collectors have never been popular, but in Jesus' time they were 'outcasts'. Fellow Jews hated paying taxes to their rulers, the Romans, and doubly so when the collectors themselves were Jewish.

> 'Once again Jesus went out beside the lake. A large crowd came to him, and he began to teach them. As he walked along, he saw Levi son of Alphaeus sitting at the tax collector's booth. "Follow me," Jesus told him, and Levi got up and followed him. While Jesus was having dinner at Levi's house, many tax collectors and "sinners" were eating with him and his disciples, for there were many who followed him. When the teachers of the law who were Pharisees saw him eating with the "sinners" and tax collectors, they asked his disciples: "Why does he eat with tax collectors and 'sinners'?" On hearing this, Jesus said to them, "It is not the healthy who need a doctor, but the sick. I have not come to call the righteous, but sinners."'
> (Mark 2:13–17)

For discussion

- Who are Jesus' critics in this passage?
- Why would Jesus eat with 'outcasts'?
- What does the final sentence suggest about the reason Jesus came to earth?

What does this say about the nature of discipleship?

- Jesus seems to make controversial choices for his first disciples – fishermen led simple lives and were unimportant; tax collectors were 'outcasts' and recognised as sinners. The jobs of these people or how they had acted in the past did not matter to Jesus. In fact, he seems to choose them because they are ordinary people.

- These five men all follow Jesus whole-heartedly and without question. They give up everything, leaving their jobs and families to become disciples.

- Jesus tells these disciples that they will become 'fishers of men'. Instead of catching fish, they will be 'catching' people so that they follow Jesus, and will be learning and spreading the word of God.

All of these things are very important for Christians today. Christians believe that they too should follow Jesus whole-heartedly and do whatever he wants them to do. They also believe that they should be 'fishers of men' and learn and spread the word of God. Like Jesus, Christians should accept everyone as disciples, no matter who they are or what they have done. What is important is that they want to follow Jesus.

Activities

7 Explain why the nature of discipleship as shown in the calling of the first disciples is important to Christians today.

Summary

Jesus starts by appointing the first disciples to be his close friends and helpers. He calls them to leave their jobs to travel and work with him. This shows that the nature of discipleship is to follow the master whole-heartedly.

1.2 Sending out the Twelve

6

Learning outcomes

By the end of this lesson, you should be able to:

- state the meaning of service
- give your own opinion, with a reason, about the nature of discipleship as shown in the sending out of the Twelve
- explain why Jesus sent out the Twelve in this way
- evaluate different points of view about how it affects ideas about Christian living today.

Activities

1 Imagine you are part of a Duke of Edinburgh Award group, preparing for your expedition. Working in pairs, make a list of the items you think are essential for your trip. Now add other items you think are important, but not essential.

Be prepared to explain your lists and justify your choices.

Young people on a Duke of Edinburgh Award expedition. You could find out more about the Duke of Edinburgh Award scheme from your school or visit the website (go to www.pearsonschoolsandfecolleges.co.uk/hotlinks (express code 4271P) and click on the appropriate link).

edexcel ⠿ key terms

Service – An act of help or assistance.

The Twelve – The twelve selected from the disciples to be Jesus' closest disciples.

The Twelve have been learning from Jesus, watching him speak to crowds and heal people. Now it was time to put their lessons into practice:

'Calling the Twelve to him, he sent them out two by two and gave them authority over evil spirits. These were his instructions: "Take nothing for the journey except a staff – no bread, no bag, no money in your belts. Wear sandals but not an extra tunic. Whenever you enter a house, stay there until you leave that town. And if any place will not welcome you or listen to you, shake the dust off your feet when you leave, as a testimony against them." They went out and preached that people should repent. They drove out many demons and anointed many sick people with diseases and healed them.' (Mark 6:7–13)

Activities

Compare your preparations in Activity 1 with the story above:

2 How do you think the preparations of the Twelve would compare with yours?

3 To avoid the possibility of accidents every precaution has to be taken on a Duke of Edinburgh Award trip, but why do you think the disciples were so restricted in what they could take?

Thinking about the instructions the Twelve were given:

4 What were they told to do?

5 What does this tell us about the nature of being a disciple?

What does this say about the nature of discipleship?

Jesus' instructions show that:

- being a disciple is about getting out and doing **service** – to work as a player, rather than a spectator
- disciples must be focused on the task, not carrying extra baggage with them
- disciples should preach wherever they go and try to stop people from sinning
- disciples should work against evil
- disciples should help sick people.

Today's disciples also need to be focused, ready to go wherever God leads, unencumbered by loads of possessions (see the story of the rich man on page 12). While Jesus chose a small group to be his first students, he taught them to make disciples of all those who wanted to become his followers. All Christians are supposed to be disciples... and that can be a problem.

Bethlehem Experience – an event in Parkland (Glasgow's East End) at Christmas time, similar to the Hope 2008 events. Churches come together to re-enact what Bethlehem would have been like when Christ was born.

Activities

6 Across the UK, churches of all sorts joined together for Hope 2008 events. The aim was to give something worthwhile to the local community, with different groups trying to arrange special days for young people or families or whoever else needed help. In some areas this led to clean-ups, where hundreds of church people went round their area picking up rubbish; others built play areas or organised fun day runs with free food and entertainment for anyone who could come along.

Explain how events like Hope 2008 show that Christians today still follow Jesus' instructions to the early disciples.

For discussion

In your groups, discuss how you think Christians today should:

- 'preach the gospel'
- care for the sick
- fight against evil and injustice.

Do you think that the type of discipleship shown in Mark is still meant for Christians today, or should Christians restrict themselves to caring for the sick and feeding the hungry? Should they restrict the preaching part to inside their church buildings and keep out of politics?

Summary

The sending out of the Twelve shows that disciples should not worry about food, clothes or money. They should rely on those who receive them. They should also preach repentance and heal the sick.

1.3 The true family of Jesus

8

Learning outcomes

By the end of this lesson, you should be able to:

● state the meaning of true family

● give your own opinion about Jesus' attitude to true family

● explain how the teachings on true family show some of the costs of discipleship

● explain how this teaching causes problems for some Christians today.

Who are the 'true family'?

Read the passage here about Jesus' reaction when his family came to call:

> 'Then Jesus' mother and brothers arrived. Standing outside, they sent someone in to call him. A crowd was sitting around him, and they told him, "Your mother and brothers are outside looking for you."
>
> "Who are my mother and my brothers?" he asked. Then he looked at those seated in a circle around him and said, "Here are my mother and my brothers! Whoever does God's will is my brother and sister and mother."' (Mark 3:31–35)

Activities

1 In pairs or threes, draw a sketch to show the incident described above. You should include one of Jesus' family outside, someone in the house listening to Jesus, and Jesus himself. How would you expect each one to react?

edexcel ⋮⋮⋮ key terms

True family – Those who follow the teachings of Jesus.

In Mark's gospel, Jesus says that a person's true family are all those who do God's will.

Jesus seems to be changing the definition of family here! He is saying that his **true family** are all those people who do God's will. Discipleship demands total dedication from those who follow. This story shows that the cost of becoming a disciple might mean giving up your related family and friends, but that being a disciple gives a person a new family made up of the followers of Jesus.

ResultsPlus
Build Better Answers

Do you think serving God is more important than loving your family?
Give **two** reasons for your point of view. (4 marks)

 Basic, 1-mark answers
These answers will give a personal opinion with one brief reason.

Good, 2–3-mark answers
2-mark answers will offer a personal opinion and either give two brief reasons or one developed reason. 3-mark answers will give one brief reason and one developed reason.

 Excellent, 4-mark answers
The best answers will give a personal opinion supported by two developed reasons.

True family for Christians today

Christians believe that the Church is God's family, so that all believers are brothers and sisters. Any human family has its stresses and strains, so that there are quarrels and bitterness dividing and separating family members. Sadly, this is also true of the Church, as it is made up of human beings too, so that some churches and communities will also be at odds with one another from time to time. The one unifying factor among Christians, as Jesus said, is to belong to his family by doing the will of God.

Being a true disciple of Jesus means that a person is a member of the Christian family. However, this might come at a cost. Living as a disciple might mean that people become distanced from their own family or friends if they are not Christians too. When someone becomes a Christian they may sometimes meet resistance from other family members – Mum or Dad perhaps. This can make it very difficult for them. In some cultures, they may have to leave the family home as a result.

For discussion

- In the passage from Mark on page 8, Christians are told that they are members of God's family if they do God's will. When they fall out with one another and go their own way, do you think they cease to be his family members?
- Do you think religious commitment can, or should, override family commitment?

Dear Christian Teen Advice,

I have recently become a Christian. I want to go to the Youth Service on Sunday evenings but my parents have told me that I have to stay in with them and if I disobey them I will be a 'bad Christian'. What should I do?

John

Activities

2 Write a reply to John's letter to a Christian teen magazine. What do you think he should do?

3 Would your advice be different if John's disagreement with his parents was over a week-long Christian camp? Why/why not?

Summary

All who 'do God's will' are members of the true family of Jesus.

1.4 True greatness

Learning outcomes

By the end of this lesson, you should be able to:

● state the meaning of true greatness

● give your own opinion about Jesus' attitude to true greatness

● explain how the costs of discipleship are shown in true greatness

● explain how this teaching causes problems for some Christians today.

Activities

1   Working in pairs, decide on the qualities that you would expect to see in a truly great person. Write a list of those qualities.

Mother Teresa ministers to the poor of Calcutta.

Mother Teresa of Calcutta (1910–1997)

"'By blood, I am Albanian. By citizenship, an Indian. By faith, I am a Catholic nun. As to my calling, I belong to the world. As to my heart, I belong entirely to the Heart of Jesus." Small of stature, rocklike in faith, Mother Teresa of Calcutta was entrusted with the mission of proclaiming God's thirsting love for humanity, especially for the poorest of the poor. "God still loves the world and He sends you and me to be His love and His compassion to the poor." She was a soul filled with the light of Christ, on fire with love for Him and burning with one desire: "to quench His thirst for love and for souls"' (from the official Mother Teresa website: www.motherteresa.org).

edexcel key terms

Self-sacrifice – Putting other people's needs before your own.

True greatness – The teaching of Jesus that service of others is true greatness.

Activities

2   Working in pairs, make a list of the qualities that Mother Teresa showed that made people think of her as truly great.

3   Compare your two lists.

What did Jesus say about true greatness?

'They came to Capernaum. When he was in the house, he asked them, "What were you arguing about on the road?" But they kept quiet because on the way they had argued about who was the greatest. Sitting down, Jesus called the Twelve and said, "If anyone wants to be first, he must be the very last, and the servant of all." He took a little child and had him stand among them. Taking him in his arms, he said to them, "Whoever welcomes one of these little children in my name welcomes me; and whoever welcomes me does not welcome me but the one who sent me."'
(Mark 9:33–37)

Many people think of Mother Teresa as exemplifying **true greatness**. Thousands from across the world mourned when she died, not just on the streets of Calcutta where she worked. She was a true servant to others.

Jesus tells the disciples that to be truly great they need to put others first and help them – this is known as **self-sacrifice**. He emphasises this by using the example of a child. A child is dependent on others, needs to be looked after, is not powerful or rich or influential. When Jesus was teaching, children had no status in Jewish society, so they represented everyone who was weak or oppressed. By welcoming a child, Jesus says that the disciple is welcoming him.

What did Jesus say about true greatness?

Activities

4 Jesus said, 'If anyone wants to be first, he must be the very last, and the servant of all.' What do you think he meant by this?

5 Explain how you think Mother Teresa put this teaching into practice.

True greatness for Christians today

It may seem that the structure of today's churches suggests an order of importance, greatness and position – for example, in the Roman Catholic Church, the Pope, archbishops, bishops and priests. However, these titles and positions are not supposed to show status, or that one person is better than another, but are intended as positions of service. Those called to 'The Ministry' or to 'Holy Orders' are supposed to serve others.

To get an idea of what this means, here is part of the Methodist Church's information for 'Ministry candidates': 'The calling of the Methodist Church is to respond to the gospel of God's love in Christ and to live out its discipleship in worship and mission.'

The words that follow are said in the Methodist service of ordination:

'In God's name you are to preach by word and deed the Gospel of God's grace;… to lead God's people in worship, prayer and service;… to serve others in whom you serve the Lord himself.… In them you are to watch over one another in love.'

The cost of true greatness

Jesus' ideas of true greatness are very different from other ideas about 'greatness' both in his own society and in society today. People are often looked up to because of what they look like or how much money they have. Jesus' teaching implies that, to become truly great, people have to give up these things and serve other people. This may cause conflict for Christians who enjoy their lifestyle and do not want to change. Some churches make more of this difference than others, and this too causes tensions.

Jesus was asking his disciples to be radically different from other people – this in itself can be difficult! Also, serving other people can be both physically and emotionally demanding.

Activities

6 'There are lots of ways to serve other people. You don't necessarily have to live like Mother Teresa.' Do you agree? Give reasons for your point of view.

Summary

True greatness in the Christian faith comes from serving others, because in that way the Christian is serving God. Many Christians find it difficult and demanding to serve.

1.5 The rich man

Learning outcomes

By the end of this lesson, you should be able to:

● state the meaning of the eye of a needle

● describe how the costs of discipleship are shown in the story of the rich man

● give your own opinion about the costs demanded of the rich man by Jesus

● explain how this teaching causes problems for some Christians today.

edexcel ⠿ key terms

The commandments – The collection of 10 laws given by God.

The eye of a needle – A metaphor used by Jesus to show that wealth makes it difficult to enter the Kingdom of God.

Activities

1 How much would you give up? In the television game *Deal or No Deal*, what would you do? Gamble or not?

The rich man

'As Jesus started on his way, a man ran up and fell on his knees before him. "Good teacher," he asked, "what must I do to inherit eternal life?"

"Why do you call me good?" Jesus answered. "No one is good – except God alone. You know **the commandments**: 'Do not murder, do not commit adultery, do not steal, do not give false testimony, do not defraud, honour your father and mother'."

"Teacher," he declared, "all these I have kept since I was a boy."

Jesus looked at him and loved him. "One thing you lack," he said. "Go, sell everything you have, give to the poor, and you will have treasure in heaven. Then come, follow me."

At this the man's face fell. He went away sad, because he had great wealth.

Jesus looked around and said to his disciples, "How hard it is for the rich to enter the kingdom of God!"

The disciples were amazed. But Jesus said again, "Children, how hard it is to enter the kingdom of God! It is easier for a camel to go through **the eye of a needle** than for a rich man to enter the kingdom of God." The disciples were even more amazed, and said to each other, "Who then can be saved?"

Jesus looked at them and said, "With man this is impossible, but not with God; all things are possible with God."

Peter said to him, "We have left everything to follow you!"

"I tell you the truth," Jesus replied, "no one who has left home or brothers or sisters or mother or father or children or fields for me and the gospel will fail to receive a hundred times as much in this present age (homes, brothers, sisters, mothers, children and fields – and with them, persecutions) and in the age to come, eternal life. But many who are first will be last, and the last first."' (Mark 10:17–31)

One of the gates in Jerusalem is called 'Needle Gate'. This cartoonist has used this to portray the eye of a needle metaphor.

Activities

2   In the Church of England, a survey showed that each member of the Church gave £5.38 weekly on average in 2006 in charity – about 3 per cent of average income (source: Church of England website: www.churchofengland.org, October 2008). While many may pay considerably more, does this show that discipleship is easy – or hard?

3   In your books, draw up a cost/benefit chart, showing advantages and disadvantages of the disciple's life. On balance, are the costs worth paying?

DISCIPLESHIP	
Costs	Benefits

What is the cost of following Jesus?

From this passage it looks like the cost of discipleship is:

• to keep the ten commandments
• to be prepared to give away all your money and everything you own. Your rewards for doing this will be a hundred times as much and eternal life.

It is unlikely that Jesus meant for everyone literally to give away everything – how would they afford to eat and drink, for example? Jesus is not saying that everyone must give up everything, although some may choose to. He says that the demands made on one person are different from those made on another. The fishermen left families and fishing to follow Jesus, but Legion (see pages 106–107) was told to go home to tell his family he had been healed.

Jesus is saying that the wealthier a person is, the more difficult it is to fully commit to being a disciple and follow God. Perhaps he means that self-sacrifice is harder when you have more to sacrifice!

The Christian Church has been criticised in the past because it has so much wealth and there are many rich Christians. Christians have to decide their priorities carefully. This is a problem for them in a society where success is often measured by the salary earned and the possessions you have.

Activities

4   Imagine a quiz show for Christians called *Disciple or Not Disciple*. What would a person have to do to win?

5   Some Christians would argue that there is nothing wrong with being rich in itself as long as you use your money to serve others. Do you agree with them?

Summary

The story of the rich young man suggests that not everyone will be able, or willing, to follow the life of a disciple. The demands are different for different people.

1.6 The tenants

Learning outcomes

By the end of this lesson, you should be able to:

● describe how the costs of discipleship are shown in the parable of the tenants

● give your own opinion, with a reason, about what Jesus meant in this story

● explain what relationship this parable has to Christians today

● evaluate different points of view about the costs shown in the story.

For discussion

● Imagine someone has criticised you in front of a crowd of people. How would you react? Would you just walk away? Would you start an argument? Would you start a fight?

● What if that person was important – your teacher, for example. Would that make a difference to your reaction?

Jesus tells a story that is seen as criticism of the Jewish leaders

An allegory is a story in which characters and events in a make-believe world represent people and events in the real world. The details may have a hidden meaning. To understand the meaning it is necessary to crack the code. There are several 'allegories' in Mark's gospel. The parable of the tenants is one of them.

'He then began to speak to them in parables: "A man planted a vineyard. He put a wall around it, dug a pit for the winepress and built a watchtower. Then he rented the vineyard to some farmers and went away on a journey. At harvest time he sent a servant to the tenants to collect from them some of the fruit of the vineyard. But they seized him, beat him and sent him away empty-handed. Then he sent another servant to them; they struck this man on the head and treated him shamefully. He sent still another, and that one they killed. He sent many others; some of them they beat, others they killed. He had one left to send, a son, whom he loved. He sent him last of all, saying, 'They will respect my son.'

'"But the tenants said to one another, 'This is the heir. Come, let's kill him, and the inheritance will be ours.' So they took him and killed him, and threw him out of the vineyard. What then will the owner of the vineyard do? He will come and kill those tenants and give the vineyard to others. Haven't you read this scripture: 'The stone the builders rejected has become the capstone; the Lord has done this, and it is marvellous in our eyes'?" Then they looked for a way to arrest him because they knew he had spoken the parable against them. But they were afraid of the crowd; so they left him and went away.'
(Mark 12:1–12)

A vineyard at harvest time – the parable of the tenants is used as an allegory in Mark's gospel.

Cracking the code

In Jesus' story:

- the owner of the vineyard represents God
- the vineyard represents the Jews
- the tenants are the Jewish leaders
- the servants are the prophets who brought God's word to the people
- the son represents Jesus, so the killing of the son would be the crucifixion, and the rejected stone, the resurrection of Jesus
- the 'others' are then the Gentiles.

Activities

1 Read through the story again. Retell it using the actual characters – you could draw a cartoon or storyboard as well as words.

At the time, Galilean peasants hated their foreign landlords, and the Zealots (a nationalist group) were stirring up a revolt against them. In the story, the tenants know the owner is abroad and so they know they can take liberties with the servants. When the son arrives, the tenants assume the owner has died and the son has come to claim his inheritance. By Jewish law, if a property has no owner, it becomes the tenants', so here the tenants kill the son to acquire the vineyard.

Most Christians today understand this story as Jesus prophesying his death. Interpreted in this way, Jesus is saying that the Jewish leaders will reject God's messengers first and then his Son, killing him. Instead of taking over, though, they will be replaced, for God's chosen people will no longer be just the Jews.

The capstone is a reference to Psalm 118, but it also has another meaning. Jesus may appear to them as worthless, but he will turn out to be the cornerstone of the building: Jesus the carpenter from Nazareth will turn out to be the Jewish Messiah. The Jewish leaders at the time would have understood what Jesus meant and so would have been very angry.

Activities

Read Psalm 118.

2 What is a capstone or cornerstone?

3 Why is this so important in the story?

4 In the allegory of the tenants, who do you think represents the disciples?

5 What were the costs to these disciples?

And what of today?

Christians today recognise that they are God's messengers bringing his word to the people. They too may face rejection or death for their faith. Jesus himself came for all people, not just his own people, the Jews, who rejected him. In the early stages of Christianity, the Church was thought of as a branch of Judaism, with Church members even meeting in the synagogues. But soon the Church spread to the Gentiles across the Roman Empire.

The parable sums up God's plan for the whole of humanity – from the creation to Jesus' death and resurrection, and on to the present, where people who believe in him can be reconciled to God.

Activities

6 Explain how the parable of the tenants is significant for some Christians today.

Summary

Jesus told a parable about the tenants of a vineyard who beat or kill the owner's servants and, finally, his son when they come to claim the owner's rights. It is an allegory that criticises the Jewish leaders, showing they will oppose God (the owner) and persecute and kill God's servants.

1.7 A spirit cast out by Jesus

Learning outcomes

By the end of this lesson, you should be able to:

● describe the story of Jesus healing the boy after the failure of the disciples

● explain how this teaching causes problems for some Christians today

● evaluate different points of view about healing and casting out evil spirits.

Activities

1 What was wrong with the boy? People in Jesus' day believed illness was due to evil spirits. Read through the passage again and list the boy's symptoms.

Some people believe that the boy was an epileptic. Epilepsy is a disorder of the nervous system. It is very disturbing for the sufferer and those nearby. Read this description of an epileptic fit: 'He fell to the ground and began to shake and twitch uncontrollably. He seemed to have trouble breathing and became pale and clammy. After two minutes, the shaking ceased and he came round, but was confused. Before the seizure he was acting quite normally – but suddenly he cried out and the seizure began.'

2 Do you think the boy that Jesus healed could have suffered an epileptic fit?

3 Does this affect your view of what Jesus did?

The failure of Jesus' disciples

'When they came to the other disciples, they saw a large crowd and the teachers of the law arguing with them. As soon as all the people saw Jesus, they were overwhelmed with wonder and ran to greet him. "What are you arguing with them about?" he asked. A man in the crowd answered, "Teacher, I brought you my son, who is possessed by a spirit that has robbed him of speech. Whenever it seizes him, it throws him to the ground. He foams at the mouth, gnashes his teeth and becomes rigid. I asked your disciples to drive out the spirit, but they could not."

'"O unbelieving generation," Jesus replied, "how long shall I stay with you? How long shall I put up with you? Bring the boy to me." So they brought him. When the spirit saw Jesus, it immediately threw the boy into a convulsion. He fell to the ground and rolled around, foaming at the mouth. Jesus asked the boy's father, "How long has he been like this?"

'"From childhood," he answered. "It has often thrown him into fire or water to kill him. But if you can do anything, take pity on us and help us."

'"If you can'?" said Jesus. "Everything is possible for him who believes."

'Immediately the boy's father exclaimed, "I do believe; help me overcome my unbelief!" When Jesus saw that a crowd was running to the scene, he rebuked the evil spirit. "You deaf and mute spirit," he said, "I command you, come out of him and never enter him again." The spirit shrieked, convulsed him violently and came out. The boy looked so much like a corpse that many said, "He's dead." But Jesus took him by the hand and lifted him to his feet, and he stood up. After Jesus had gone indoors, his disciples asked him privately, "Why couldn't we drive it out?" He replied, "This kind can come out only by prayer."' (Mark 9:14–29)

Jesus has given his disciples the power to cast out demons (Mark 3:15) but they have not succeeded in this case. When Jesus returns he seems angry with them and blames lack of faith. He says that they have not understood the true meaning of prayer. It seems that Jesus expected more from his disciples. That is a problem for them.

Jesus performs many healing miracles in Mark's gospel, but in this topic he has to do it because the disciples have failed – that is the important part to remember.

In this 15th-century manuscript the artist has recreated the story of Jesus casting out a spirit. Can you identify which characters are which? How does the artist do this?

Activities

4   Draw up a storyboard from the time Jesus joined the crowd.

5   Imagine you were there. Working in fours, each person chooses one of the characters – the father, the son, a disciple or Jesus. Think about your feelings. Replay the scene.

For Christians today

Some people might believe that Jesus really did drive evil spirits out of the boy, while some would say that the boy had a mental illness (or epilepsy, as discussed opposite).

Christians might also be concerned because, if even the disciples were unable to act on Jesus' instructions, how can ordinary people today follow his teachings properly?

For discussion

Jesus obviously believed he was dealing with an evil spirit, and cast it out of the boy. Some Christians still believe that there are such things. What do you think?

Summary

The disciples failed Jesus and were unable to heal a boy brought to them. Jesus then healed the boy, teaching the disciples to pray for the healing.

1.8 The parable of the sower

Learning outcomes

By the end of this lesson, you should be able to:

- describe how the problems of discipleship are shown in the parable of the sower (Mark 4:1–20)

- give your own opinion about Jesus' explanation of the parable

- evaluate different points of view about the problems caused by this story for some Christians today.

edexcel ⋯ key terms

The kingdom – The rule of God in people's lives.

'Again Jesus began to teach by the lake. The crowd that gathered around him was so large that he got into a boat and sat in it out on the lake, while all the people were along the shore at the water's edge. He taught them many things by parables, and in his teaching said: "Listen! A farmer went out to sow his seed. As he was scattering the seed, some fell along the path, and the birds came and ate it up. Some fell on rocky places, where it did not have much soil. It sprang up quickly, because the soil was shallow. But when the sun came up, the plants were scorched, and they withered because they had no root. Other seed fell among thorns, which grew up and choked the plants, so that they did not bear grain. Still other seed fell on good soil. It came up, grew and produced a crop, multiplying thirty, sixty, or even a hundred times." Then Jesus said, "He who has ears to hear, let him hear."

'When he was alone, the Twelve and the others around him asked him about the parables. He told them, "The secret of **the kingdom** of God has been given to you. But to those on the outside everything is said in parables so that, 'they may be ever seeing but never perceiving, and ever hearing but never understanding; otherwise they might turn and be forgiven!'" Then Jesus said to them, "Don't you understand this parable? How then will you understand any parable? The farmer sows the word. Some people are like seed along the path, where the word is sown. As soon as they hear it, Satan comes and takes away the word that was sown in them. Others, like seed sown on rocky places, hear the word and at once receive it with joy. But since they have no root, they last only a short time. When trouble or persecution comes because of the word, they quickly fall away. Still others, like seed sown among thorns, hear the word; but the worries of this life, the deceitfulness of wealth and the desires for other things come in and choke the word, making it unfruitful. Others, like seed sown on good soil, hear the word, accept it, and produce a crop – thirty, sixty or even a hundred times what was sown."'
(Mark 4:1–20)

Jesus gives an allegorical interpretation of the parable that shows the four kinds of soil representing different types of hearer of Jesus' message. It is the only parable in any of the gospels that has an interpretation included. Some people think that the Church may have added the interpretation to Mark's gospel in early times to explain how different groups of people responded to God's kingdom. They think this because it seems to go against their ideas of how Jesus taught people.

Jesus is therefore telling the disciples that different people will react differently to their work. Not everyone will respond positively to the Christian message that they are spreading, and this is one of the problems of discipleship.

This parable would have encouraged Christians – it is thought that Mark was writing for those followers who were being persecuted by the Roman emperor Nero. Large numbers of Christians were being tortured and killed because of their beliefs. Many had been thrown to the lions in the arena and others were used as human torches to light the streets. All this made some question their faith.

The footpath represents the one who does not listen – Satan carries off the word before the hearer responds.

The rocky ground represents the shallow hearer – this person has no roots, lacks depth and therefore has no persistence.

The thorny ground represents the worldly hearer – the person who is attracted by the pleasures of the world.

The fertile soil represents the responsive listener – the person who puts their faith into practice and lives fruitfully.

Mark wrote of those seeds landing on rocky ground withering because they have no root. The person who claims to believe but is not really committed will not stay when the pressure of persecution comes.

Activities

1   In Jesus' day most people would have been familiar with stories from farming, so they would have quickly picked up on the parable of the sower. Today, though, more people live in towns and cities and have no experience of the countryside, so how do you think Jesus would teach this lesson now? Retell the story for today's 'townies'.

Why does Mark's account cause problems for today's Christians?

All of the types of people Jesus is describing in this parable may still be relevant for today.

There are still parts of the world where Christians face persecution for their faith, and there are still people who are represented by the footpath or the rocky ground, who either do not want to hear Jesus' message or do not become dedicated followers. The thorny ground may be particularly relevant in today's wealthy world where there are so many distractions.

The problem is that Mark's account does not offer a solution to these problems – what are Christians to do when the Christian message does not get through to people?

There are other problems with Mark's account. Some people do not believe that Mark wrote the explanation of this parable – if this is the case then it might not be an accurate account of what Jesus meant. Also, according to Mark in this passage, Jesus did not want sinners to understand his parables because he did not want them to repent and be forgiven. This seems to contradict all his teachings in other parts of the gospels about coming to call sinners to repentance. Jesus may have explained the parable, or the gospel writers used it as a teaching device.

Activities

2   Explain how the four different types of people described in the parable may still be relevant today.

Summary

The sower is an allegory that tells how God's kingdom grows and how different people respond to the message. Jesus' interpretation speaks of the effect on people's faith 'when trouble or persecution comes'.

1.9 Jesus, the disciples and service

20

Learning outcomes

By the end of this lesson, you should be able to:

● describe Jesus' teaching on service

● give your own opinion, with a reason, about what Jesus meant in this story

● explain what problems this raises for Christian disciples

● evaluate different points of view about what this means for Christians today.

To help with the background to this passage, read this section from earlier in the chapter about James and John:

'Then James and John, the sons of Zebedee, came to him. "Teacher," they said, "we want you to do for us whatever we ask."

'"What do you want me to do for you?" he asked.

'They replied, "Let one of us sit at your right and the other at your left in your glory."

'"You don't know what you are asking," Jesus said. "Can you drink the cup I drink or be baptised with the baptism I am baptised with?"

'"We can," they answered. Jesus said to them, "You will drink the cup I drink and be baptised with the baptism I am baptised with, but to sit at my right or left is not for me to grant. These places belong to those for whom they have been prepared."' (Mark 10:35–40)

Apparently, James and John wanted to have a special place with Jesus in his kingdom. They thought they had earned it, but Jesus has to correct them. Read on:

'When the ten heard about this, they became indignant with James and John. Jesus called them together and said, "You know that those who are regarded as rulers of the Gentiles lord it over them, and their high officials exercise authority over them. Not so with you. Instead, whoever wants to become great among you must be your servant, and whoever wants to be first must be slave of all. For even the Son of Man did not come to be served, but to serve, and to give his life as a ransom for many."' (Mark 10:41–45)

The Pope symbolises Christ's humility. One of the titles of the Pope is Servus Servorum Dei – *the Servant of the Servants of God.*

who work together to provide food for the homeless in the evenings. For example, Bristol Soup Run Trust was founded in 1986 by Pip'n'Jay's Church (an Anglican church) and the Bristol Cyrenians.

Jesus taught that his disciples (all Christians) should serve others. Many Christians do this today by working for organisations that provide help for those who need it.

In this passage, Jesus explains to James and John that his followers will not have a special place of authority as the Romans did. We have already seen that 'greatness' for Jesus is not about political power and wealth, but that instead it is about serving others (see pages 10–11). In this passage, Jesus goes even further and says that the person who is first must be a slave to everyone else.

What does Jesus mean by the final line? A ransom is a sum of money or other request that is demanded by someone holding people prisoner. Christians believe that people are prisoners of sin. Therefore Jesus is once again predicting his own death, but this time he is explaining why he has to die. His death will be the ultimate example of serving others – dying for other people.

These types of service can be tiring and difficult in their own ways, but there are many examples of Christians who have followed Jesus' ultimate example of service and have willingly given up their own lives for others.

ResultsPlus
Build Better Answers

What does **service** mean? (2 marks)

⬤ **Good, 1-mark answers**
These will give a partly correct definition of the term.

▲ **Excellent, 2-mark answers**
These will give a short, accurate definition.

What do the teachings in this passage mean for Christians today?

Service to others is one of the costs of discipleship. It can be difficult to put other people first, but this teaching is a reminder to Christians today that in following Jesus they must be prepared to serve others. An example of service can be found in churches and other Christian groups across Britain

Summary

Jesus taught his disciples that they must serve others to be considered great by God.

1.10 Are the disciples really failures?

Learning outcomes

By the end of this lesson, you should be able to:

● describe the failure of the disciples

● give your own opinion, with a reason, about the problems of discipleship shown in their failure

● explain how this teaching could be both a help and a problem for Christians living today

● evaluate different points of view about what this means for Christians today.

The Garden of Gethsemane today.

After Jesus had finished eating the Last Supper (see pages 62–65) with his disciples, he took them out to the Mount of Olives. They were on their way to the Garden of Gethsemane where they could spend some time together. Jesus started with a warning. It is a quote from Zechariah – an Old Testament book written a little more than 500 years before Jesus.

> '"You will all fall away," Jesus told them, "for it is written: 'I will strike the shepherd, and the sheep will be scattered.' But after I have risen, I will go ahead of you into Galilee."
>
> 'Peter declared, "Even if all fall away, I will not." "I tell you the truth," Jesus answered, "today – yes, tonight – before the rooster crows twice you yourself will disown me three times." But Peter insisted emphatically, "Even if I have to die with you, I will never disown you." And all the others said the same.' (Mark 14:27–31)

These are brave words from Peter. All too soon he will regret saying them.

> 'They went to a place called Gethsemane, and Jesus said to his disciples, "Sit here while I pray." He took Peter, James and John along with him, and he began to be deeply distressed and troubled. "My soul is overwhelmed with sorrow to the point of death," he said to them. "Stay here and keep watch." Going a little farther, he fell to the ground and prayed that if possible the hour might pass from him. "Abba, Father," he said, "everything is possible for you. Take this cup from me. Yet not what I will, but what you will."' (Mark 14:32–36)

Jesus appears worried. He is praying to his Father about the situation that he knows is about to occur. He has asked his close disciples, Peter, James and John, to stay with him, but they do not understand what is happening.

> 'Then he returned to his disciples and found them sleeping. "Simon," he said to Peter, "are you asleep? Could you not keep watch for one hour? Watch and pray so that you will not fall into temptation. The spirit is willing, but the body is weak." Once more he went away and prayed the same thing. When he came back, he again found them sleeping, because their eyes were heavy. They did not know what to say to him. Returning the third time, he said to them, "Are you still sleeping and resting? Enough! The hour has come. Look, the Son of Man is betrayed into the hands of sinners. Rise! Let us go! Here comes my betrayer!"' (Mark 14:37–42)

Just when he needs them most, the disciples have fallen asleep. They have let him down three times by falling asleep instead of supporting him in prayer.

Activities

1 Make a list of the things Jesus told his disciples to do in this passage from the time they reach Gethsemane. Tick the parts they actually achieved.

2 From your list, how do you think they failed Jesus?

3 How do you think Jesus felt
   • as he prayed
   • as he came to his disciples?

4 Write down the words that would show his feelings.

How does this both help and cause problems for Christians today?

Christians are human beings and sometimes they may get tired and forget to pray or simply put it off for another occasion. In doing this they are behaving rather as Jesus' disciples did when they fell asleep in the Garden of Gethsemane. However, trying not to fail in this way is one of the duties of all Christians.

When people find it difficult to maintain the duties of their faith they may be encouraged when they remember that the first disciples faced difficult challenges and sometimes failed to live up to what was asked of them. They may also remember that it was these same disciples who turned their failure into success by spreading the word and establishing the Christian Church. People may feel that this success helps them to face challenge and persecution today. They may also be comforted by the idea that, although Jesus was disappointed with the disciples, he showed his understanding when he said, 'The spirit is willing, but the body is weak.'

For discussion

• The Christians to whom Mark was writing were facing persecution in Rome. How might this story have helped them?

• Christians in the UK face little in the way of persecution, so how do you think they may be encouraged by this story? Surely failure is not good, is it?

Summary

Jesus took his disciples to the Garden of Gethsemane. He asked his closest three friends, Peter, James and John, to support him but they fell asleep – three times. They failed to support him through this crisis, and yet the Christian Church exists today because of their work after Jesus' death.

1.11 Peter denies knowing Jesus

24

Learning outcomes

By the end of this lesson, you should be able to:

- describe Peter's denial of Jesus and how the problems of discipleship are shown (Mark 14:66–72)
- give your own opinion, with a reason, about why Peter responded as he did
- explain how this story could be a help to Christians today
- evaluate different points of view about how it may cause problems for Christians living today.

edexcel ⋮⋮⋮ key terms

Peter's denial – The way Peter said he was not a follower of Jesus after the arrest of Jesus.

Have you ever been faced with a tricky situation in which you were frightened to tell the truth? In such situations it often seems safer to tell a lie, or at least not to tell the whole truth. Not many of us would be in the sort of danger that Peter was facing here, though.

Peter's hero, Jesus, had been arrested and was on trial in the High Priest's house. Only a short time earlier, when they had come out to the Mount of Olives following the Last Supper, Peter had promised Jesus that he would never desert him. We saw this in the last topic (page 22), so read Jesus' words again, along with Peter's response.

Not very long after this, Jesus has been betrayed by Judas and taken off to trial. Peter wants to find out what is going on, but it is dangerous for him. Will the guards be looking to round up Jesus' followers? Now he finds himself in the courtyard outside the High Priest's house, trying to look inconspicuous. A servant girl recognises him – his cover is blown. What should he say? If he tells the truth, will he be arrested? Should he play it safe?

'While Peter was below in the courtyard, one of the servant girls of the high priest came by. When she saw Peter warming himself, she looked closely at him. "You also were with that Nazarene, Jesus," she said. But he denied it. "I don't know or understand what you're talking about," he said, and went out into the entryway.

'When the servant girl saw him there, she said again to those standing around, "This fellow is one of them." Again he denied it. After a little while, those standing near said to Peter, "Surely you are one of them, for you are a Galilean." He began to call down curses on himself, and he swore to them, "I don't know this man you're talking about."

'Immediately the rooster crowed the second time. Then Peter remembered the word Jesus had spoken to him: "Before the rooster crows twice you will disown me three times." And he broke down and wept.' (Mark 14:66–72)

The Denial of St Peter *(c1525–1530)* by the *16th-century Flemish illustrator Simon Bening. Who is Peter in this image? Analyse the painting to see what the artist is saying about the event and Peter himself.*

Activities

1 Write a summary of what happened in the High Priest's courtyard.

For discussion

Were the disciples failures?

petr? flevit amar

What does this mean?

On the face of it, at this stage the way of discipleship has ended in failure. All twelve disciples have run away, leaving Jesus to face his trial and execution all on his own. Peter, the one person Jesus might have expected to stand by him, has denied even knowing him.

Perhaps this is to show that the way of discipleship is hard and costly; perhaps, also, that discipleship is not just about following Jesus but also about believing and trusting in him, too. The Church exists today because those disciples who let Jesus down became convinced that he had risen from the dead and then went on to spread the word across the world.

Today, many Christians find this view of discipleship helpful. They may feel that they cannot understand all Jesus' teaching. They may have failed and deserted Jesus, but knowing that those who were closest to Jesus could still do this encourages them to struggle on as Christians.

Peter's denial of knowing Jesus occurred because he was scared of being arrested himself. Disciples today may not face the same life-or-death issues, but they may be faced with tricky decisions. At work, for example, should they tell the truth to their boss and face getting the sack, or should they 'bend the truth a little' to keep their job safe? In some circumstances they may be asked to compromise their faith and 'deny Jesus' themselves. In recent cases in the UK, the authorities have challenged workers who have shared their faith, either by wearing crosses or saying prayers with clients.

Activities

2 Think of some situations where Christians might be tempted to deny being a Christian. What might they do? What should they do?

Summary

Peter followed Jesus to just outside the High Priest's house, but denied knowing Jesus when challenged by a servant girl. He denied it three times, leaving Jesus unsupported.

KnowZone
Discipleship

Quick quiz

1 Who were the Sons of Zebedee?

2 What was Levi's job?

3 Who were the Twelve?

4 Who are Jesus' true family?

5 What is true greatness?

6 How many commandments are there? Can you name two?

7 What is 'the eye of a needle'?

8 What is the kingdom?

9 What is the difference between self-sacrifice and service?

10 Who denied knowing Jesus?

Plenary activity

Design an ideas map of all the different topics in this section on discipleship. The one here has been started to give you some help.

Find out more

The following books are good places to find out more:

- *Mark's gospel – An Interpretation for Today* by Robin Cooper (Hodder, ISBN 0-340-43029-X)

- *Mark: A Gospel for Today* 3rd ed by Simon and Christopher Danes (St Mark's Press, ISBN 9-781-9070-6200-1)

- *Revise GCSE Religious Studies* (Letts, ISBN-13 9-781-8431-5515-7)

You can also find out more in the Christianity section of the BBC's Religion website. Go to www. pearsonschoolsandfecolleges.co.uk/hotlinks (express code 4271P) and click on the appropriate link.

Student tips

I found it really useful to teach the revision topic, for example 'The rich man meets Jesus', to a friend or member of my family. I was then able to find out whether I could explain it properly to them. This is really helpful in answering the third question on the exam where you have to explain why or how the story causes problems to modern Christians.

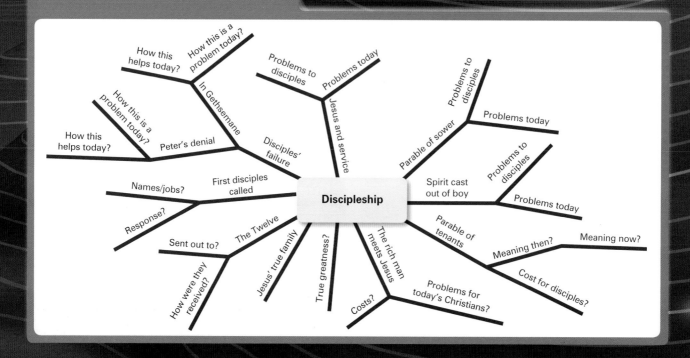

Self-evaluation checklist

How well have you understood the topics in this section? In the first column of the table below use the following code to rate your understanding:

Green – I understand this fully.

Orange – I am confident I can answer most questions on this.

Red – I need to do a lot more work on this topic.

In the second and third columns you need to think about:

- whether you have an opinion on this topic and could give reasons for that opinion if asked
- whether you can give the opinion of someone who disagrees with you and give reasons for this alternative opinion.

Content covered	My understanding is red/orange/green	Can I give my opinion?	Can I give an alternative opinion?
How the nature of discipleship is shown in the call of the first disciples			
Why this is important for Christians today			
How the nature of discipleship is shown in the sending out of the Twelve			
How this affects ideas about Christian living today			
How the costs of discipleship are shown in the true family of Jesus			
Why this teaching causes problems for some Christians today			
How the costs of discipleship are shown in true greatness			
Why this teaching causes problems for some Christians today			
How the costs of discipleship are shown in the rich man			
Why this teaching causes problems for some Christians today			
How the costs of discipleship are shown in the parable of the tenants			
The relationship between the parable of the tenants and Christians today			
How the problems of discipleship are shown in the spirit cast out of the boy			
Why this teaching causes problems for some Christians today			
How the problems of discipleship are shown in the parable of the sower			
Why Mark's account causes problems for Christians today			
How the problems of discipleship are shown in Jesus and service			
What this means for Christian living today			
How the problems of discipleship are shown in the failure of the disciples			
How this might both help and cause problems for Christians today			
How the problems of discipleship are shown in Peter's denial			
How this might both help and cause problems for Christians today			

KnowZone
Discipleship

Introduction

In the exam you will see a choice of two questions on this section. Each question will include four tasks that test your knowledge, understanding and evaluation of the material covered. A 2-mark question will ask you to define a term; a 4-mark question will ask you to give your opinion on a point of view; an 8-mark question will ask you to explain a particular belief or idea; a 6-mark question will ask for your opinion on a point of view and ask you to consider an alternative point of view.

Here you need to give a short, accurate definition. You do not need to write more than one clear sentence.

The important words in the question are 'explain why', so you must make sure that this is what you focus on in your answer. This is worth 8 marks so you must be prepared to spend some time answering it. You will also be assessed on your use of language in this question.

Now you must give the opposite point of view. As before, give reasons you have learned in class. You must show you understand why people have these other views, even if you don't agree with them.

Mini exam paper

(a) What are **disciples**? (2 marks)

(b) Do you think Peter was a failure?

Give **two** reasons for your point of view. (4 marks)

(c) Explain why the story of the rich man might cause problems for some Christians today. (8 marks)

(d) 'It is much easier to be a disciple of Jesus today.'

In your answer you should refer to Mark's gospel and Christianity.

(i) Do you agree? Give reasons for your opinion. (3 marks)

(ii) Give reasons why some people may disagree with you. (3 marks)

You must give your opinion but make sure you do give two clear and properly thought-out reasons. These can be ones you have learned in class.

In your answer you should state whether you agree with the statement, and you need to support your opinion with reasons.

Mark scheme

(a) You can earn **2 marks** for a correct answer, and **1 mark** for a partially correct answer.

(b) To earn up to the full **4 marks** you need to give two reasons and develop them. Two brief reasons or only one developed reason will earn **2 marks**.

(c) You can earn **7–8 marks** by giving up to four reasons, but the fewer reasons you give, the more you must develop them. Because you are being assessed on use of language, you also need to take care to express your understanding in a clear style of English and make some use of specialist vocabulary.

(d) To go beyond **3 marks** for the whole of this question you must refer to Christianity and Mark's gospel. The more you are able to develop your reasons, the more marks you will earn. Three simple reasons can earn you the same mark as one fully developed reason.

ResultsPlus
Build Better Answers

(b)　Do you think Peter was a failure? Give **two** reasons for your point of view. (4 marks)

Student answer	Comments	Improved student answer
Peter was a failure because he denied being a follower of Jesus outside the High Priest's house when Jesus was arrested. A disciple should not have done this. He had also run away when Jesus was arrested.	The student's first paragraph gives a developed reason, worth 2 marks. The second paragraph is a brief reason, worth 1 further mark. To gain full marks, the student needs to develop the second reason.	Peter was a failure because he denied being a follower of Jesus outside the High Priest's house when Jesus was arrested. A disciple should not have done this. When Jesus needed the disciples to support him and stay with him at the time of his arrest, Peter and the other disciples deserted him.

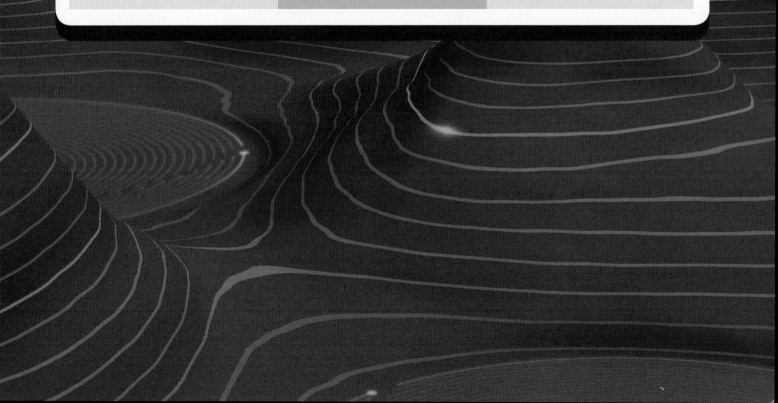

Conflict and argument

Introduction

The purpose of this section is to help you investigate how Jesus ran into conflict with the religious authorities as a result of his teaching and his actions. You will explore the causes for argument and the conflict and problems that arose. The disciples misunderstood Jesus from time to time, and that also led to conflict.

> ### Learning outcomes for this section
>
> By the end of this section, you should be able to:
>
> - give definitions of the key words and use them in answers to GCSE questions
> - describe how the healing of the paralysed man led to conflict and explain its significance for Christians today
> - describe how the disagreements about the Sabbath led to conflict and explain their significance for Christians today, particularly in relation to current issues of social and community cohesion
> - describe how disagreements about the meaning of the Law led to conflict and explain their significance for Christians today, particularly in relation to current issues of social and community cohesion
> - describe why Jesus' predictions of his Passion might have led to conflict and explain their significance for Christians today
> - describe why Jesus' entry into Jerusalem might have caused conflict and explain its significance for Christians today
> - describe why Jesus' cleansing of the Temple might have caused conflict and explain its significance for Christians today, particularly in relation to current issues of social and community cohesion
> - describe how the argument about authority might have led to conflict and explain its significance for Christians today
> - describe how Jesus' answer to the question about Caesar and taxes might have led to conflict and explain its significance for Christians today, particularly in relation to current issues of social and community cohesion
> - describe how Jesus' argument with the Sadducees about resurrection might have led to conflict and explain its significance for Christians today
> - describe why the anointing at Bethany might have led to conflict and explain its significance for Christians today
> - explain the meaning and significance of the plot to kill Jesus.

edexcel ▦ key terms

| corban | the Law | Passion | ritual cleanliness | Sadducees | sinners |
| fasting | Palm Sunday | Pharisees | Sabbath | scribes | the Temple |

The Merchants Chased from the Temple by Christ (c1850).

Jonathan Edwards, Olympic, Commonwealth, European and World Champion Triple Jumper.

1 The picture above shows the most famous scene of conflict and argument presented in the gospels. Does this image surprise you? How is it different from other portrayals of Jesus?

Christian Eric Liddell – as seen in the film *Chariots of Fire* (1981) – refused to run in the 100 metres final in the 1934 Paris Olympics, as it took place on a Sunday. More recently, Jonathan Edwards (left) also refused to compete on a Sunday because of his strong Christian beliefs, although he later changed his mind.

In both cases these men were in conflict with the authorities because their faith told them they should keep Sunday as a day of rest. As the UK's multi-faith society grows, so it becomes more common for those holding a religious faith to be in conflict with that society. Working or competing on a Sunday is just one example.

2 Is there some activity that you would refuse to take part in because your conscience told you not to? Discuss this in pairs.

2.1 Jesus heals a paralysed man

32

Learning outcomes

By the end of this lesson, you should be able to:

● describe the story of Jesus healing the paralysed man

● explain why Jesus' action caused offence to the teachers of the Law

● express your own opinions about Jesus' action

● give your opinion on who Christians believe is qualified to forgive sins.

edexcel ⠿ key terms

the Law – The collection of laws handed down by God and collected in the Torah.

sinners – Those who did not follow all the Jewish laws.

Activities

1 How important was faith in the healing of the paralysed man?

2 Whose faith was it that brought about the healing, and how was it shown?

The first conflict involving Jesus takes place when he heals a paralysed man:

'A few days later, when Jesus again entered Capernaum, the people heard he had come home. So many gathered there was no room left, not even outside the door, and he preached the word to them. Some men came, bringing to him a paralytic, carried by four of them. Since they could not get him to Jesus because of the crowd, they made an opening in the roof above Jesus and, after digging through it, lowered the mat the paralyzed man was lying on. When Jesus saw their faith, he said to the paralytic, "Son, your sins are forgiven."

'Now some teachers of the law were sitting there, thinking to themselves, "Why does this fellow talk like that? He's blaspheming! Who can forgive sins but God alone?"

'Immediately Jesus knew in his spirit that this was what they were thinking in their hearts, and he said to them, "Why are you thinking these things? Which is easier: to say to the paralytic, 'Your sins are forgiven,' or to say, 'Get up, take your mat and walk'? But that you may know that the Son of Man has authority on earth to forgive sins…" He said to the paralytic, "I tell you, get up, take your mat and go home." He got up, took his mat and walked out in full view of them all. This amazed everyone and they praised God, saying, "We have never seen anything like this!"' (Mark 2:1–12)

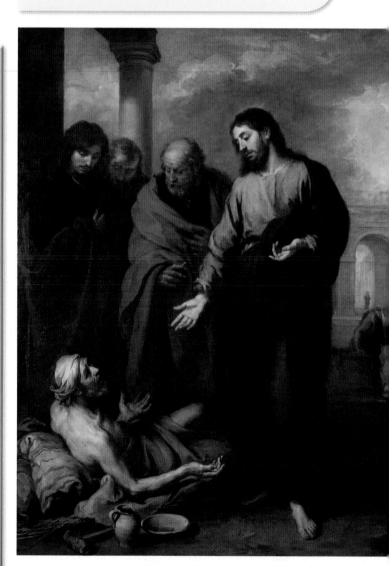

Christ Healing the Paralytic at the Pool of Bethesda *(late 1660s) by Bartolome Esteban Murillo.*

Why did this healing lead to conflict?

Jesus did something surprising when the men brought the man to him. He said his sins were forgiven. In the Jewish faith, it was thought that disease was caused by demons or by sin. A Jewish teacher wrote that a person could not be healed of a sickness until all their sins were forgiven. Probably the paralysed man believed this, so Jesus reassured him.

The religious authorities believed only God could forgive a **sinner**. By saying that the man's sins were forgiven, Jesus was seen as insulting God, or claiming to be God. This was the most serious religious offence – blasphemy.

Jesus knew why the teachers of **the Law** were offended, so he showed them that he had the authority by asking which was easier – to forgive sins or to tell the man to get up and walk. He finished by telling the paralytic to get up, take his mat and go home, which he did.

What is the significance of this healing for Christians today?

In the story of Jesus sending out the Twelve (see pages 6–7) he gave them authority to forgive sins and heal. Christians believe that that authority and power remains with the Church. Roman Catholic priests have authority to hear people's confessions. They usually do this in the church in a 'confessional'. Having heard the confession, the priest can forgive the person.

A confessional box in a Catholic church. The priest sits in one side, the person making their confession in the other. A small grille between allows them to speak but not to see one another.

Christians believe that Jesus, as part of God, still has the power to heal people, and they pray for this to happen. Many Christians believe that churches also have authority to heal people. Some churches anoint a person with oil and pray for healing. There are claims that many are healed (although not everyone). This may pose a problem for some Christians today, because some people are healed while others are not.

ResultsPlus
Build Better Answers

Do you think priests have the right to forgive a person's sins?

Give **two** reasons for your point of view. (4 marks)

 Basic, 1-mark answers
Students who get one mark will give their opinion but with just one brief reason.

 Good, 2–3-mark answers
2-mark answers will give an opinion with either one developed reason or with two brief reasons. 3-mark answers will give one brief and one developed reason for the student's opinion.

 Excellent, 4-mark answers
Students who get full marks for this question will give their opinion with two developed reasons.

For discussion

- What was the problem for the teachers of the Law?
- What was Jesus claiming?
- What does this mean for Christians today?

Summary

When Jesus told a paralysed man that his sins were forgiven, the religious leaders saw this as blasphemy, because they believed that only God could forgive sins. Christians today pray for forgiveness and healing.

2.2 Disagreements about the Sabbath

Learning outcomes

By the end of this lesson, you should be able to:

- describe conflicting views about the Sabbath
- explain why these disagreements led to a problem for the Pharisees
- express your own opinions about how the Sabbath should be observed
- give your point of view, with reasons, about how this relates to issues of social and community cohesion.

One of the Ten Commandments says:

'Remember the **Sabbath** day by keeping it holy. Six days you shall labour and do all your work, but the seventh day is a Sabbath to the LORD your God. On it you shall not do any work, neither you, nor your son or daughter, nor your manservant or maidservant, nor your animals, nor the alien within your gates. For in six days the LORD made the heavens and the earth, the sea, and all that is in them, but he rested on the seventh day. Therefore the LORD blessed the Sabbath day and made it holy.' (Exodus 20:8–11)

Activities

1 Go to www.pearsonschoolsandfecolleges.co.uk/ hotlinks (express code 4271P) and click on the link to find out more about the Sabbath and then list what is not permitted on the Jewish Sabbath.

2 Why do you think this commandment says that people should do no work on the Sabbath? What exactly does 'no work' mean?

Now read about the trouble Jesus and his disciples had when they went for a walk in the fields:

edexcel ::: key terms

Pharisees – A religious group whose aim was to keep the traditional Jewish faith alive.

Sabbath – The Jewish day of rest on the seventh day of the week.

'One Sabbath Jesus was going through the grainfields, and as his disciples walked along, they began to pick some heads of grain. The **Pharisees** said to him, "Look, why are they doing what is unlawful on the Sabbath?"

'He answered, "Have you never read what David did when he and his companions were hungry and in need? In the days of Abiathar the high priest, he entered the house of God and ate the consecrated bread, which is lawful only for priests to eat. And he also gave some to his companions." Then he said to them, "The Sabbath was made for man, not man for the Sabbath. So the Son of Man is Lord even of the Sabbath."' (Mark 2:23–28)

Jesus gets into further trouble as he goes to synagogue one Sabbath day:

'Another time he went into the synagogue, and a man with a shrivelled hand was there. Some of them were looking for a reason to accuse Jesus, so they watched him closely to see if he would heal him on the Sabbath. Jesus said to the man with the shrivelled hand, "Stand up in front of everyone." Then Jesus asked them, "Which is lawful on the Sabbath: to do good or to do evil, to save life or to kill?" But they remained silent.

'He looked around at them in anger and, deeply distressed at their stubborn hearts, said to the man, "Stretch out your hand." He stretched it out, and his hand was completely restored. Then the Pharisees went out and began to plot with the Herodians how they might kill Jesus.' (Mark 3:1–6)

The Lame Man Reaches out to Jesus, 14th-century mosaic. Jesus causes conflict because he heals a man's withered hand on the Sabbath – this would have been seen as 'working' on the Sabbath, which was not allowed according to Jewish law.

Activities

3 Explain what Jesus and his disciples had done wrong, according to the Pharisees in both of these stories.

How did Jesus respond to the Pharisees?

In the first story Jesus talked about an Old Testament incident where the Jews' greatest king, David, broke the Sabbath law to feed his hungry troops. Jesus' argument was that human need is more important than keeping a law, and besides that, as he was God's representative, he had the authority to break the law anyway. In the second story he showed that he was not restricted by the limitations of the Law if he could 'do good' and 'save life'.

How do Christians respond today?

There is still disagreement among Christians about what they are allowed to do on the Sabbath. To some people today, Christians seem to be like the Pharisees, saying, 'you can't do this or that on a

Sunday'. Other Christians, such as those working for the Keep Sunday Special campaign, believe that they do not have to keep this law strictly but that Sunday should be different from other days, not just for religious reasons:

> We believe in having time for family, friends and community. We believe in time to rest and enjoy ourselves. We believe in working hard and living life to the full.
>
> And we believe in keeping just one day a week a bit special.
>
> **Keep Sunday Special campaign website**

The problem is that the UK is a multi-faith society made up of people with many different beliefs. This raises lots of questions:

- Members of some other faiths also have special days or times during the week – Saturdays for Jews, for example. Does this mean that these other days should be 'special days' too?
- What happens when religious duties interfere with your job? What happens if your employer says you have to work on a 'holy day'?
- What about people who don't follow a religious faith – how should they respond to people's requests based on religious teachings or laws?

Jesus' message in this story is that human need is more important than keeping religious laws. This is an important message for social and community cohesion.

For discussion

Should Sunday be treated differently from other days of the week?

Summary

Disagreements about the Sabbath led to conflict for Jesus and his disciples, and continue to lead to debate among Christians today, particularly in relation to shops opening on Sundays.

2.3 The trouble with the Law (1)

Learning outcomes

By the end of this lesson, you should be able to:

- describe the problem caused by Jesus eating a meal with his disciples

- explain why it was a problem to the Pharisees

- explain what Jesus meant in his reply about corban

- give your opinion on its significance to Christians today, particularly in relation to current issues of social and community cohesion.

edexcel ::: key terms

fasting – Going without food on certain days as a sign of devotion to God.

ritual cleanliness – The Jewish laws on food and washing which prevented anything unclean entering the body.

A kosher kitchen. Orthodox Jews have their kitchens divided into two sections – one for meat and the other for milk products. In these there will be separate utensils, crockery and cutlery. This fulfils the Jewish food laws.

Activities

1 Do you have any special things you do before a meal – set the table, maybe, or wash your hands? If you were serving a meal for someone important, how would you make the meal special?

A kosher certificate. This shows a food product is permitted for Jews to eat.

The Pharisees were very strict about many things, as they felt they had to protect the Law and make it fit every need of daily life. By Jesus' time they had recognised 613 points of law that, among many other things, covered how the Sabbath should be marked to the last detail and how food should be eaten.

The Pharisees were very careful to wash their hands and their food bowls and pans before eating to show, through their **ritual cleanliness**, how dedicated they were to God. Their ceremony of washing involved pouring a cup of water down from the fingers to the elbow, so that any contact they had made during the day with ordinary Jews, or Gentiles, would be cleansed. In their desire to protect the Law, the Pharisees also focused on **fasting** – going without food on certain days to show God how devoted they were.

Now read the story where Jesus is having a meal with his disciples:

'The Pharisees and some of the teachers of the law who had come from Jerusalem gathered around Jesus and saw some of his disciples eating food with hands that were "unclean," that is, unwashed. (The Pharisees and all the Jews do not eat unless they give their hands a ceremonial washing, holding to the tradition of the elders. When they come from the marketplace they do not eat unless they wash. And they observe many other traditions, such as the washing of cups, pitchers and kettles.)

'So the Pharisees and teachers of the law asked Jesus, "Why don't your disciples live according to the tradition of the elders instead of eating their food with 'unclean' hands?" He replied, "Isaiah was right when he prophesied about you hypocrites; as it is written: 'These people honour me with their lips, but their hearts are far from me. They worship me in vain; their teachings are but rules taught by men.' You have let go of the commands of God and are holding on to the traditions of men."' (Mark 7:1–8)

In the minds of the Pharisees, Jesus is disobeying the food laws and is therefore being disrespectful to God.

How did Jesus respond to the criticisms of the Pharisees?

Jesus quoted from Isaiah, the Old Testament prophet, to suggest that the Pharisees merely paid lip-service to God as they worshipped him only superficially. He called them hypocrites who pretended to be better than they really were – showing how religiously observant they were, but not really caring for God. He argued that they had taken the rules to the extreme and forgotten why they should follow God's Law.

Activities

2 What does Jesus mean by 'You have let go of the commands of God and are holding on to the traditions of men'? How do you think Christians would interpret this?

For discussion

Do you think Jesus was right to sit down to eat without first performing the ritual washing?

2.3 The trouble with the Law (2)

Jesus went further in his criticism of the Pharisees:

'And he said to them: "You have a fine way of setting aside the commands of God in order to observe your own traditions! For Moses said, 'Honour your father and your mother,' and, 'Anyone who curses his father or mother must be put to death.' But you say that if a man says to his father or mother: 'Whatever help you might otherwise have received from me is Corban' (that is, a gift devoted to God), then you no longer let him do anything for his father or mother. Thus you nullify the word of God by your tradition that you have handed down. And you do many things like that."

'Again Jesus called the crowd to him and said, "Listen to me, everyone, and understand this. Nothing outside a man can make him 'unclean' by going into him. Rather, it is what comes out of a man that makes him 'unclean.'"

'After he had left the crowd and entered the house, his disciples asked him about this parable. "Are you so dull?" he asked. "Don't you see that nothing that enters a man from the outside can make him 'unclean'? For it doesn't go into his heart but into his stomach, and then out of his body." (In saying this, Jesus declared all foods "clean.")

'He went on: "What comes out of a man is what makes him 'unclean.' For from within, out of men's hearts, come evil thoughts, sexual immorality, theft, murder, adultery, greed, malice, deceit, lewdness, envy, slander, arrogance and folly. All these evils come from inside and make a man 'unclean.'" (Mark 7:9–23)

Jesus continued to attack the Pharisees for setting up their own traditions that went against the Ten Commandments, which Jews believed were the basis for their faith. He chose this example – 'Honour your father and your mother' – which would require them to love and respect their parents, being prepared to care for them in practical ways as they got older. By swearing that

edexcel key terms

corban – A gift dedicated to God which meant that it could not be used for anything else.

his goods were dedicated to God a person would then not be able to use his money or possessions to help his parents. This was the practice of **corban**.

Activities

3 Christians do not follow the Jewish food laws because of what Jesus says in this passage. Explain why.

ResultsPlus
Build Better Answers

Explain why Jesus and the Pharisees came into conflict over the Law. (8 marks)

■ **Basic, 1–2-mark answers**
Answers which get low marks will give one simple reason.

● **Good, 3–6-mark answers**
Level 2 answers (3–4 marks) will give two brief reasons, or a developed reason. Level 3 answers (5–6 marks) will give three brief reasons, or a fully developed reason, or one simple reason and one developed reason.

▲ **Excellent, 7–8-mark answers**
Most excellent answers will show clear understanding of the issue by using four brief reasons, or two developed reasons, or two simple reasons and one developed reason, or a comprehensive explanation using one fully developed reason.

Significance for Christians today

The list of thoughts Jesus mentions as coming from inside a person to make them unclean are still thought to be wrong today, as they were in Jesus' time. They are all things that involve abusing others and as such degrade those people. Christians believe that every human being, whether Christian or not, should be treated with respect, as the faith is concerned with human dignity and the worth of every human relationship. The Christian faith should have nothing to do with anything that abuses or misuses another person for profit or greed, because these things separate people from God and from each other.

Corban

Corban is a gift or offering consecrated to God. Anything over which this word was once pronounced was dedicated to the temple. If you chose to give some land, however, this could be redeemed before the Year of Jubilee (Leviticus 27:16–24). Jesus condemned the Pharisees saying that by their traditions they had destroyed the commandment that requires children to honour their father and mother. One of the Ten Commandments is to honour your father and mother but by allowing and encouraging people to give corban, the Pharisees are stopping people from looking after their parents.

sexual immorality

greed

folly

lewdness

slander

adultery

envy

theft

murder

malice

deceit

arrogance

Activities

7   What do you think Jesus meant when he criticised the Pharisees here?

8   Explain what Jesus meant by uncleanness.

Activities

4   Read the words above and find out what they mean. Write down the definitions in your books.

5   Looking at the list, are there some that you think are no longer 'evil'? Why?

6   How do you think members of other faiths would view these evil thoughts?

Summary

The Pharisees and other Jewish leaders saw Jesus' disciples eating a meal without going through the ritual washing and they questioned him. Other disagreements about the meaning of the Law also led to conflict. Christians today are called to treat all people with respect and dignity and not to abuse or misuse others for profit or greed.

2.4 Jesus predicts his Passion

40

Learning outcomes

By the end of this lesson, you should be able to:

● describe the teaching of Jesus predicting his Passion

● explain why Peter was upset about this

● express your own opinions about why this might have led to conflict

● give your opinion on the significance of this teaching to Christians today.

There are several occasions in Mark's gospel where Jesus speaks about what is going to happen to him. The first time this happens, it leads to conflict with Peter:

> 'He then began to teach them that the Son of Man must suffer many things and be rejected by the elders, chief priests and teachers of the law, and that he must be killed and after three days rise again. He spoke plainly about this, and Peter took him aside and began to rebuke him. But when Jesus turned and looked at his disciples, he rebuked Peter. "Get behind me, Satan!" he said. "You do not have in mind the things of God, but the things of men."'
> (Mark 8:31–33)

Just before this, Peter had told Jesus he believed that Jesus was the Messiah, the Christ (see pages 96–97), but now Jesus uses his preferred title: the 'Son of Man'. The disciples believed they were following a 'Messiah' who would defeat the Romans and bring in a time of peace and freedom. When Jesus told them that he was going to be killed, it must have seemed to the disciples that he had just given up. They would not have understood this teaching about rising from the dead, as the idea of resurrection would have been new to the Jews. This is why Peter tells Jesus off!

Jesus' response to Peter seems harsh, but he needed to get the message across to him and the other disciples that this is God's plan. It seems that their ideas about the Messiah as a warrior king are not part of this plan.

edexcel ::: key terms

Passion – The sufferings of Jesus, especially in the time leading up to his crucifixion.

Activities

1 Imagine you have been following Jesus but that now he says these things about rejection and death. How would you feel?

2 Why do you think Jesus called Peter 'Satan' in this passage?

ResultsPlus
Top Tip!

This passage is used for more than just this topic! Make sure you learn it carefully, as you may be able to use it in your answers to several different exam questions.

Now read the other passages where Jesus predicts his **Passion**:

> 'They left that place and passed through Galilee. Jesus did not want anyone to know where they were, because he was teaching his disciples. He said to them, "The Son of Man is going to be betrayed into the hands of men. They will kill him, and after three days he will rise." But they did not understand what he meant and were afraid to ask him about it.'
> (Mark 9:30–32)

> 'They were on their way up to Jerusalem, with Jesus leading the way, and the disciples were astonished, while those who followed were afraid. Again he took the Twelve aside and told them what was going to happen to him. "We are going up to Jerusalem," he said, "and the Son of Man will be betrayed to the chief priests and teachers of the law. They will condemn him to death and will hand him over to the Gentiles, who will mock him and spit on him, flog him and kill him. Three days later he will rise."' (Mark 10:32–34)

Most Christians today believe that Jesus rose from the dead after three days. According to Mark, Jesus predicted what was going to happen and everything took place as he said. Christians believe that God knows everything that has happened and everything that is going to happen. Therefore, Christians see Jesus' predictions of what was going to happen as further evidence that Jesus is God's son.

This 5th- to 6th-century mosaic in Ravenna, Italy, portrays Jesus as a warrior. This is more in keeping with the traditional idea of the Jewish Messiah as a soldier who would battle for freedom.

Activities

3 Write down the things that these three predictions have in common and then the things that are different.

4 Explain why Jesus' predictions of his Passion may have led to conflict.

Challenge

In all three of the stories on page 40, Jesus made predictions about his forthcoming Passion. There are two ways to view these predictions.

- First, that they are actually Jesus' own words of prophecy, with Jesus having supernatural insight into what is due to happen to him.

- The alternative view is that Mark wrote these predictions with the benefit of hindsight, using them to underline the significance of Jesus' suffering and death.

What do you think?

Summary

In these three stories, Jesus predicted his Passion – his suffering and death. This led to conflict with Peter when he tried to correct Jesus. The teaching about the suffering and death of Jesus is very important for Christians today as it explains the events that followed.

2.5 Jesus enters Jerusalem

Learning outcomes

By the end of this lesson, you should be able to:

- describe the events of Palm Sunday
- explain why Jesus' entry into Jerusalem might have caused conflict
- express your own opinions about the significance of this for Christians today.

edexcel ::: key terms

Palm Sunday – The Sunday before Good Friday when Jesus entered Jerusalem on a donkey.

Now read how Jesus began his final week leading up to the crucifixion:

The Entry into Jerusalem *(c1303–1305)* by Giotto. Why might Jesus' entry into Jerusalem have caused conflict?

'As they approached Jerusalem and came to Bethphage and Bethany at the Mount of Olives, Jesus sent two of his disciples, saying to them, "Go to the village ahead of you, and just as you enter it, you will find a colt tied there, which no one has ever ridden. Untie it and bring it here. If anyone asks you, 'Why are you doing this?' tell him, 'The Lord needs it and will send it back here shortly.'"

'They went and found a colt outside in the street, tied at a doorway. As they untied it, some people standing there asked, "What are you doing, untying that colt?" They answered as Jesus had told them to, and the people let them go. When they brought the colt to Jesus and threw their cloaks over it, he sat on it. Many people spread their cloaks on the road, while others spread branches they had cut in the fields. Those who went ahead and those who followed shouted, "Hosanna! Blessed is he who comes in the name of the Lord! Blessed is the coming kingdom of our father David! Hosanna in the highest!"

'Jesus entered Jerusalem and went to the Temple. He looked around at everything, but since it was already late, he went out to Bethany with the Twelve.' (Mark 11:1–11)

Activities

1 Start to make a timeline or wall chart to show the events of the last week of Jesus' life as recorded by Mark. Begin with Jesus' entry into Jerusalem.

Why Jesus' entry into Jerusalem might have led to conflict

As he rode into Jerusalem on a colt, Jesus appeared to be showing that he was the Messiah. The Old Testament prophet Zechariah had written about the coming of the Messiah in this way, 'humble and mounted on an ass' (Zechariah 9:9). Mark quoted Psalm 118:25–26, 'Blessed is he who comes in the name of the Lord!' – a common greeting for any pilgrim entering Jerusalem, and there is also a link with King David. Jesus was coming to Jerusalem in the way the prophets had foretold.

The Jewish leaders would have seen the arrival of Jesus in Jerusalem in this way as a threat to their authority. He was welcomed by the crowds, and the leaders may well have expected him to lead a rebellion after this show of his popularity. No doubt they would have been familiar with the words of the Psalm and would have made the connection between Jesus and prophecies about the Messiah.

The early Church soon came to believe that Jesus had intended to be a peaceful Messiah, not a military leader (see pages 110–111) and so started the celebration of **Palm Sunday**.

Activities

2 What instructions did Jesus give when he sent the disciples to collect the colt (donkey)?

3 What do you think the story of Jesus' entry into Jerusalem means?

4 Divide a page into two columns. In the left-hand column write down what happened in the story. In the right-hand column write down what each part teaches about Jesus.

What happened as Jesus rode into Jerusalem?	What does this teach about Jesus?

Activities

5 In groups, act out Jesus' entry into Jerusalem, accompanied by two or three disciples, with some passers-by.

6 How do you imagine a Jewish priest would view Jesus' arrival in Jerusalem?

The significance of Jesus' entry into Jerusalem for Christians today

Many Christians see Jesus' entry into Jerusalem as fulfilling Old Testament prophecies about the Messiah and as showing who Jesus was. Jesus was greeted as a king while he was riding the animal of a poor person, and some Christians may see this as making Jesus approachable and humble and a role model for both rich and poor.

Christians now look forward to Jesus' Second Coming as a time that will come when they 'will see the Son of Man coming in clouds with great power and glory' (Mark 13:26) (see page 113). In response to this, some Christians recently placed a webcam on the Mount of Olives to watch for Jesus' return, but later the view was restricted by building works.

For discussion

Why do you think the story of Jesus' entry into Jerusalem is important to Christians today?

Summary

Jesus came to Jerusalem on a colt, with crowds throwing palm branches in his path. The people shouted, 'Hosanna! Blessed is he who comes in the name of the Lord!' They believed that their Messiah had come. Christians today worship Jesus, the Messiah.

2.6 Jesus clears out the Temple

Learning outcomes

By the end of this lesson, you should be able to:

- describe Jesus' actions in cleansing the Temple
- explain what Jesus meant by describing the Temple as 'my house'
- describe some of the ways in which the Temple had been made 'a den of robbers'
- explain the significance for Christians today, particularly in relation to current issues of social and community cohesion.

Activities

1   St Paul's Cathedral in London, along with many other large religious buildings, charges an entry fee for the thousands of tourists who visit every year. Do you think it is right to do this? Discuss this with your partner and be prepared to justify your answer.

Now read about Jesus' action when he entered **the Temple** in Jerusalem:

'On reaching Jerusalem, Jesus entered the temple area and began driving out those who were buying and selling there. He overturned the tables of the money changers and the benches of those selling doves, and would not allow anyone to carry merchandise through the temple courts. And as he taught them, he said, "Is it not written: 'My house will be called a house of prayer for all nations'? But you have made it 'a den of robbers.'" The chief priests and the teachers of the law heard this and began looking for a way to kill him, for they feared him, because the whole crowd was amazed at his teaching.' (Mark 11:15–18)

edexcel ▦ key terms

the Temple – The building in Jerusalem where sacrifices were made.

This is a model of how the Temple would probably have looked in Jesus' time.

The Western (or Wailing) Wall is all that remains of the Temple today.

Why was Jesus angry?

Jesus believed that the Temple, which was the centre of Jewish worship, had been misused. The Court of the Gentiles – the only part open to non-Jews – had been taken over for two main activities: to sell animals for the sacrifices that Jewish people had to make in the Temple, and to change money. Jesus had spoken out against his opponents before, but here he used physical violence for the only time recorded in the gospel.

He quoted from the Old Testament book of Isaiah (56:7b), '...my house will be called a house of prayer for all nations', and then adds Jeremiah's words, 'Has this house, which bears my Name, become a den of robbers to you?' (Jeremiah 7:11a).

Jesus was offended that the Temple had been used as a place to make money. The Jewish leaders had come to think that the kingdom of God should be restricted to the Jewish believers, but here Jesus was including Gentiles too.

The money changers charged people who were going to the Temple to change their money for the special Temple money required to buy the sacrifices they would need in order to worship. Roman coins would show the heads of the emperors, who were regarded by the Romans as gods, so those coins could not be used. The dove sellers had a scheme where they sold worshippers the birds they would need to sacrifice, but these birds might not always be in the best condition, as the Law required. Jesus was angry about these ways in which people were misusing God's house.

So why were the Jewish leaders upset?

The Jewish leaders would have understood that Jesus' action was one of the first actions traditionally expected of the Jewish Messiah. Knowing their scriptures, they would make the connection between his action and the prophecy of Malachi, which says:

> '"See, I will send my messenger, who will prepare the way before me. Then suddenly the Lord you are seeking will come to his temple; the messenger of the covenant, whom you desire, will come," says the Lord Almighty.' (Malachi 3:1)

Activities

2 What in his clearing of the Temple showed that Jesus was including non-Jews in the kingdom?

3 Imagine you are a member of the Sanhedrin (the supreme council at Jerusalem) after Jesus has cleansed the Temple. Write the report you will give to the newspapers explaining your group's reaction to Jesus' actions.

4 Why do you think the chief priests and teachers of the Law looked for a way to kill Jesus after he had driven out those who had bought and sold in the Temple?

'A house of prayer for all nations'

Jesus spent his whole life as a Jew. By saying 'my house will be called a house of prayer for all nations' and including the part of the Temple where Gentiles were allowed, not just the Jewish section, he is making an important point for Christians today. Jesus is saying that everyone – whatever their nationality, culture, religion or race – should be treated the same. His 'house' (Christianity) is open to everyone.

Activities

5 Why do people see Jesus' words and actions here as very relevant for issues of social and community cohesion today? Explain your answer.

For discussion

How do you think charging for entry to religious buildings might affect believers? Also, many religious buildings, such as St Paul's, have shops inside that are designed to raise money for the upkeep of the buildings. Do you think that shops like this would offend Jesus in the same way as he was offended in the Temple?

Summary

Jesus found that people were not showing respect in the Temple and his actions caused conflict. His response challenges Christians today, particularly in relation to current issues of social and community cohesion.

2.7 Who's in authority here?

Learning outcomes

By the end of this lesson, you should be able to:

- describe the incident where Jesus was asked about his authority
- express your own opinions about why this might have led to conflict
- explain the reason that the religious authorities would not answer Jesus
- give your opinion on the significance of the incident for Christians today.

Activities

1. Continue with the timeline or wall chart (as begun on pages 42–43) to show the events of the last week of Jesus' life as recorded by Mark. Make a note of what Jesus had been doing in the Temple since he arrived in Jerusalem – both his actions and his words.

edexcel ::: key terms

> **Scribes ('Teachers of the Law')** – Religious lawyers; originally men who made copies of the Torah.

Read this section to find how Jesus answered a trick question about authority:

> 'They arrived again in Jerusalem, and while Jesus was walking in the temple courts, the chief priests, the teachers of the law and the elders came to him. "By what authority are you doing these things?" they asked. "And who gave you authority to do this?"
>
> 'Jesus replied, "I will ask you one question. Answer me, and I will tell you by what authority I am doing these things. John's baptism – was it from heaven, or from men? Tell me!"

Jesus and the Pharisees *(1660) by Jacob Jordaens. How has the artist portrayed the Pharisees in this painting? Do you think he was right to show them this way?*

> 'They discussed it among themselves and said, "If we say, 'From heaven,' he will ask, 'Then why didn't you believe him?' But if we say, 'From men'…" (They feared the people, for everyone held that John really was a prophet.) So they answered Jesus, "We don't know."
>
> 'Jesus said, "Neither will I tell you by what authority I am doing these things."' (Mark 11:27–33)

The Jewish leaders thought Jesus was a troublemaker. They decided that they would have to get rid of him somehow. They agreed that the best chance was to trap him into saying something that would get him arrested.

This first attempt came from the members of the Sanhedrin – Pharisees and **scribes** – who had been challenged by Jesus as he cleansed the Temple. The question they asked seemed reasonable enough: '… who gave you authority to do this?' (Mark 11:28). However, it was not altogether harmless, for if Jesus had said he had his authority from God they could charge him with blasphemy, and to claim his own authority would have led people to make fun of him. If he had said that no one had given him the right, they would have said he had acted unlawfully.

His response, however, was clever, for he challenged them to answer another question before he would answer them. This was a favourite way for Jews to debate difficult issues, for it put the pressure to answer on the other person.

> 'So Jesus said, "I will ask you one question. John's baptism – was it from heaven, or from men? Tell me!"' (Mark 11:30)

This gave them a problem, for John the Baptist had been very popular and had believed himself that he was sent to announce the arrival of the Messiah. The leaders could not answer, for that would have meant admitting that Jesus was the Messiah, and so they had to let him go.

Activities

2 Imagine you are one of the religious leaders. Describe your reaction to Jesus when he has evaded your question.

The significance of this event for Christians today

For Christians today, this incident can raise many questions about their relationship with government and its laws. Should Christians always obey the law or are they obliged to disobey it if they feel that the law goes against Christian teachings and principles? In the same way, what happens if a government makes a decision such as going to war and Christian members of the armed forces believe that this particular war is unchristian? Should they risk punishment or losing their jobs rather than ignoring their beliefs? The question is: who has the true authority – the secular world or God?

For discussion

- By whose authority do you think Jesus was doing these things?
- Christians in the government try to keep Christian standards in society. The Church of England has bishops who are members of the House of Lords. As we live in a multi-faith society some people are opposed to them having this influence on the government. They ask the question of Christians, 'Who gives you authority to do this?' How do you think Christians should answer?

Summary

When the religious leaders asked Jesus a trick question about authority, it led to conflict. The leaders could not answer Jesus' reply, so he would not answer them either. The question still applies to Christians today – by whose authority do they speak?

2.8 A taxing question

Learning outcomes

By the end of this lesson, you should be able to:

- describe the incident where Jesus is questioned about paying taxes
- explain what is meant by 'give to Caesar what is Caesar's'
- describe some of the ways in which a person can 'give to God what is God's'
- give your own point of view about the significance of this for Christians today, particularly in relation to current issues of social and community cohesion.

Roman coin showing the Emperor's head.

Activities

1 Continue with the timeline or wall chart to show the events of the last week of Jesus' life as recorded by Mark. This time focus on who asked the question and why this question was dangerous for Jesus.

'Later they sent some of the Pharisees and Herodians to Jesus to catch him in his words. They came to him and said, "Teacher, we know you are a man of integrity. You aren't swayed by men, because you pay no attention to who they are; but you teach the way of God in accordance with the truth. Is it right to pay taxes to Caesar or not? Should we pay or shouldn't we?"

'But Jesus knew their hypocrisy. "Why are you trying to trap me?" he asked. "Bring me a denarius and let me look at it." They brought the coin, and he asked them, "Whose portrait is this? And whose inscription?"

'"Caesar's," they replied. Then Jesus said to them, "Give to Caesar what is Caesar's and to God what is God's." And they were amazed at him.' (Mark 12:13–17)

Taxes were high and this reminded the Jews that their country was occupied by the Romans. The money would be paid in Roman coins stamped with a picture of the head of the Emperor. To the Jewish people, this would be against God's Law, which banned images (see Deuteronomy 4:16 and 25 and 5:8–9). In 6 CE there was a revolt against paying the tax led by a Zealot named Judas of Galilee.

Activities

2 Find out what is meant by tithing. How did it begin and how is it observed by Christians today? How might this be seen as an example of giving 'to God what is God's'?

Significance for Christians today

Mark's account was important for his original readers because they needed to know how to behave towards a non-Christian government, and Jesus' words are also important for Christians in the UK today, as the UK is multi-faith.

Some people argue that when Jesus said: 'Give to Caesar what is Caesar's and to God what is God's' (Mark 12:17), he was saying that Christians should not mix religion with politics, while others suggest that his words meant the opposite.

On the one hand, Christians were told to obey the government and not get involved with politics. The Apostle Paul also wrote about this. He said that: 'Everyone must submit himself to the governing authorities, for there is no authority except that which God has established' (Romans 13:1a). He even included the payment of taxes, explaining:

'This is also why you pay taxes, for the authorities are God's servants, who give their full time to governing. Give everyone what you owe him: If you owe taxes, pay taxes; if revenue, then revenue; if respect, then respect; if honour, then honour.' (Romans 13:6–7)

On the other hand, some people believe that Jesus was saying that God's laws are more important than a government's laws, so that Christians should be involved in politics to try to ensure the government makes laws that are in line with God's will. Those following this view would argue that God would not have approved of the Nazi government in Germany during the Second World War. These Christians believe they should obey God first if there is a clash between government and God.

One famous example of a Christian who did this is Dietrich Bonhoeffer. He was a Christian pastor who spoke out against Nazism and was involved in many resistance activities, including plotting to kill Hitler. He was executed on 9 April 1945.

Activities

3 Can you think of a situation where these Christians' views are causing conflict (in terms of social or community cohesion) in the UK today?

4 How might Christians try to resolve that conflict, following Jesus' advice?

5 What do you think would happen if people were allowed to stop paying taxes if they disagreed with the government?

6 Imagine you are a lawyer who has to defend a client who has refused to pay their tax. Prepare your case for the defence.

Summary

Jesus was challenged by a Pharisee trying to trick him into saying something against the Roman authorities. The answer 'give to Caesar what is Caesar's' tells Christians today that they should pay their taxes, and 'give to God what is God's' tells them to treat God with respect.

The US President Barack Obama is just one example of a Christian politician today. Do you think this story about taxes in Mark would encourage Christians to get involved in politics or not?

2.9 Jesus' argument with the Sadducees

Learning outcomes

By the end of this lesson, you should be able to:

- describe the story told by the Sadducees
- explain what is meant by Moses' teaching on resurrection
- express your own views about how that might have led to conflict
- explain the significance of this for Christians today.

Activities

1 Look at the inscriptions on Christian tombstones. Do the words suggest any belief in life after death? If so, what beliefs are shown?

What Christian beliefs are represented here?

edexcel ⠿ key terms

Sadducees – Group of priests who controlled the Temple and collaborated with the Romans.

The **Sadducees,** along with the Pharisees, were members of the ruling Jewish council, the Sanhedrin. They were priests and were often very wealthy. As such, they enjoyed their high position in society and would not want anything to disturb their power, particularly where the Roman authorities were concerned. Unlike the Pharisees, they collaborated (went along) with the occupying Romans.

The Sadducess took their religious and moral teaching from the Torah – the Law of Moses – but not the oral law that explained the Torah (the written law). They had little faith in the teaching of the prophets.

This meant that, unlike the Pharisees, they would not accept any teachings about resurrection after death. They also rejected the belief in the coming of a Messiah, particularly if it was one who would liberate the people from the Romans. They feared anything that would lead to conflict with Rome.

'Then the Sadducees, who say there is no resurrection, came to him with a question. "Teacher," they said, "Moses wrote for us that if a man's brother dies and leaves a wife but no children, the man must marry the widow and have children for his brother. Now there were seven brothers. The first one married and died without leaving any children. The second one married the widow, but he also died, leaving no child. It was the same with the third. In fact, none of the seven left any children. Last of all, the woman died too. At the resurrection whose wife will she be, since the seven were married to her?"

'Jesus replied, "Are you not in error because you do not know the Scriptures or the power of God? When the dead rise, they will neither marry nor be given in marriage; they will be like the angels in heaven. Now about the dead rising – have you not read in the book of Moses, in the account of the bush, how God said to him, 'I am the God of Abraham, the God of Isaac, and the God of Jacob'? He is not the God of the dead, but of the living. You are badly mistaken!'" (Mark 12:18–27)

Activities

2   In pairs, one of you take the role of a Pharisee and the other of a Sadducee. Together, write about 100 words to explain why Jesus' teaching and actions were so upsetting.

What is resurrection?

Resurrection is the belief that there is life after death, and the Pharisees taught that this would take place at the Last Day when the world would end and judgement would come. In this story, Jesus is questioned by Sadducees, who did not believe in any life after death, in an attempt to trick him. Many people thought that life after death would be very much like life on earth. Jesus dismissed the argument as a misunderstanding of God's power and the Scriptures. In the new life, there would not be marriage because, he said, it would be very different from life on earth.

What does the Old Testament teach about this?

The original story was written in Deuteronomy 25:5–6, but Jesus points the Sadducees to a passage in the Torah where God speaks to Moses from the burning bush, saying: 'I am the God of Abraham, the God of Isaac, and the God of Jacob' (Exodus 3:6). These three were the patriarchs of the Jewish faith and were dead by the time of Moses, and yet God says, 'I am', not 'I was', their God. Jesus was saying the Patriarchs are alive when he said, 'He is not the God of the dead, but of the living' (Mark 12:27).

This implies that resurrection happens immediately after death, and not on the Last Day. This also suggests that life after death is not dependent on Christian belief, as Jesus spoke of resurrection happening before he was raised. At a stroke, then, Jesus has managed to question the teachings of both the Sadducees and the Pharisees by interpreting the Scriptures they thought they alone could explain. Just imagine someone saying to your RE teacher, 'Are you not in error because you do not know the Scriptures or the power of God?'!

The significance of this for Christians today

Jesus made it very clear that there was a life after death and also that it would be a different life from that which people live on Earth. This gives hope to all Christians that when they die they will go to be with God in heaven. It also reassures them that any suffering they experience on Earth will end when they die.

Build Better Answers

Who were the **Sadducees**? (2 marks)

● **Good, 1-mark answers**
These give a partly correct answer.

▲ **Excellent, 2-mark answers**
These will give a short, accurate explanation (such as the one on page 50).

Activities

3   Look up the Bible passages in Exodus 3:6 and Deuteronomy 25:5–6. Explain in as much detail as you can how these passages relate to the argument between the Sadducees and Jesus.

4   Why do you think some Christians do not discuss what life after death will be like?

Summary

Jesus was questioned about resurrection by the Sadducees. This led to conflict at the time and has significance for Christians today because they believe that Jesus rose from the dead.

2.10 Expensive perfume at Bethany

Learning outcomes

By the end of this lesson, you should be able to:

● describe the anointing of Jesus at Bethany

● explain what was meant by the anointing

● express your own opinions about the quote, 'The poor you will always have with you.'

● give your opinion on why this action might have caused conflict

● explain why this is important to Christians today.

Clive Christian No. 1 Imperial Majesty sells at £115,000 per bottle. It is a limited edition of a Clive Christian signature scent. Sold simply as No. 1, the fragrance is priced at around £1,450 an ounce. The reason Clive Christian No. 1 Imperial Majesty costs so much is that the British designer-turned-perfumer poured 16.9 ounces of No. 1 into a Baccarat crystal bottle, placed a five-carat diamond into the 18-carat gold collar and unveiled it at Harrods in London and Bergdorf Goodman in New York City. Of the five bottles released for sale, three were sold.

Activities

1 If you were rich, would you be prepared to spend a lot of money to show you cared for someone?

The world's most expensive perfume – Clive Christian No. 1 Imperial Majesty. Only ten bottles of the scent were made.

'While he was in Bethany, reclining at the table in the home of a man known as Simon the Leper, a woman came with an alabaster jar of very expensive perfume, made of pure nard. She broke the jar and poured the perfume on his head.

'Some of those present were saying indignantly to one another, "Why this waste of perfume? It could have been sold for more than a year's wages and the money given to the poor." And they rebuked her harshly.

'"Leave her alone," said Jesus. "Why are you bothering her? She has done a beautiful thing to me. The poor you will always have with you, and you can help them any time you want. But you will not always have me. She did what she could. She poured perfume on my body beforehand to prepare for my burial. I tell you the truth, wherever the gospel is preached throughout the world, what she has done will also be told, in memory of her."' (Mark 14:3–9)

This Simon does not appear anywhere else in the gospels, so all that is known about him is that he was a leper, which would have separated him from Jewish society. Jesus was again mixing with outcasts.

So what was the woman doing? She was pouring a very expensive perfume – made from nard, a plant that grows in the Himalayas – over Jesus' head. Polite hosts would pour a little perfume on guests as they arrived at the house as a sign of welcome. It would show they valued their guests' visit. This woman used the whole jar, showing how much she valued Jesus.

Jesus gave it further meaning – families and friends would anoint a body when someone died, breaking the jar so that it could not be used again, and placing the pieces in the tomb with the corpse. The woman's action was a prophetic sign of what would happen to Jesus.

Thirdly, the title 'Messiah' means 'anointed one', and here Jesus' head was anointed by the woman. Mark reminds his readers that Jesus' death was his greatest act as the Messiah.

And what was the trouble with a woman pouring perfume over Jesus' head? First, what a waste of money! The King James Version of the Bible says that the perfume cost 'more than 300 pence' – in the version used here (New International Version) 'more than a year's wages'. How much better would it have been if it was sold to raise money for the poor?

Secondly, this woman was being over-familiar with the rabbi. What rabbi would allow a woman to do this to him? In any case, her actions could be misinterpreted. Jesus explained her actions to the critics, but her actions would certainly still cause conflict.

Why are Jesus' comments and actions important to Christians today?

Here Jesus spoke again about his death. This was the most important act of the Messiah, according to Mark, and many people believe this today. Jesus the Messiah had to suffer and to die. Once more, this gives hope to Christians and can strengthen their beliefs.

However, it is also significant that the other people in the story are Simon the Leper and the woman with the nard. Jesus is again seen associating with outcasts and women. Christians today should be prepared to follow Jesus' example. For some Christians, Jesus' attitude towards women, including having them as friends, has strengthened the argument that women should be allowed to become priests.

For discussion

'The woman had no right to anoint Jesus.' What do you think?

Summary

A woman poured expensive perfume over Jesus' head at the house of Simon the Leper. This caused conflict with other people at the house as they felt it was a waste. Jesus explained that she had done what she could to prepare his body for burial. His reply is important for Christians today, as it predicted his death.

Activities

2   What do you think Jesus meant by his reply: 'The poor you will always have with you'?

3   In groups, replay the scene with Jesus at the meal, accompanied by two or three disciples and other guests. The woman comes in and pours the perfume over his head.

2.11 The plot to kill Jesus

Learning outcomes

By the end of this lesson, you should be able to:

● describe the plot to kill Jesus

● express your own opinions about why the religious authorities wanted to arrest Jesus and kill him

● explain the significance of the plot.

Activities

1   Finish the timeline or wall chart to show the events of the last week of Jesus' life as recorded by Mark. Note down where Jesus went and what happened each day.
    It appears that he may have spent each evening at Bethany. Why do you think he would do that?

'Now the Passover and the Feast of Unleavened Bread were only two days away, and the chief priests and the teachers of the law were looking for some sly way to arrest Jesus and kill him. "But not during the Feast," they said, "or the people may riot."'
(Mark 14:1–2)

'Then Judas Iscariot, one of the Twelve, went to the chief priests to betray Jesus to them. They were delighted to hear this and promised to give him money. So he watched for an opportunity to hand him over.' (Mark 14:10–11)

'When evening came, Jesus arrived with the Twelve. While they were reclining at the table eating, he said, "I tell you the truth, one of you will betray me – one who is eating with me." They were saddened, and one by one they said to him, "Surely not I?" "It is one of the Twelve," he replied, "one who dips bread into the bowl with me. The Son of Man will go just as it is written about him. But woe to that man who betrays the Son of Man! It would be better for him if he had not been born."'
(Mark 14:17–21)

Jesus is becoming a nuisance to the religious authorities. What can they do about him?

Jesus annoyed the Jewish leaders by criticising their teachings. We have already seen that their feelings against Jesus were growing stronger. Now they wanted to silence him for good.

However, they did not want to do this during the Feast of Passover. This is because an arrest during the Feast would have been very public and Jesus was popular with many people, so they feared what the reaction might be. This is why they were delighted when Judas decided to betray Jesus to them – Judas would know where Jesus was when he left the city and this would give them a chance to arrest Jesus away from the public.

There are several ideas as to why Judas decided to betray Jesus. Some suggest that he wanted to force Jesus' hand to make him fight the Romans, as Judas expected the Messiah to do. Perhaps he had become disillusioned when Jesus showed no sign of fighting and acted out of bitterness. Other people have suggested that Judas told the chief priests that Jesus claimed to be the Messiah who would lead a rebellion against the Romans. This may have been the case, for the disciples had not at first grasped Jesus' view of what a Messiah should be.

Activities

2   Why do you think the religious authorities wanted to kill Jesus? Use what you have learned throughout this section in your answer.

What is the significance of the plot to kill Jesus?

Yet again, Jesus demonstrates that he knows exactly what is going to happen to him and those around him. He knows there is a plot going on and that one of his friends will betray him, and yet he does nothing to stop it. For Christians, this is further evidence that Jesus is God's son and that his death was all part of God's plan.

The disciples were horrified when Jesus predicted that one of them would betray him. They all ask, 'Surely not I?' (Mark 14:19). By including this, Mark showed that even Jesus' closest followers were not totally sure that they would not betray him. Peter came close when he denied him, and most Christians, then and now, might have something in their lives that makes them uneasy in Jesus' presence. It is not something to despair about, for those same disciples went on to become the first leaders of the Church. So if they could be uncertain, so can modern Christians.

The Pact of Judas *(1308–1311) by Duccio. Judas agrees to betray Jesus for 30 pieces of silver.*

In Matthew's gospel, Judas is shown as a greedy man who wanted money – he asks what the priests will give him for betraying Jesus. The money is less important in Mark's version. The 30 pieces of silver mentioned in Matthew would not have been generous, being the cost of a slave. Both Matthew and John's gospels claim that Judas was possessed by Satan, but John says that he was a thief chosen by God. We will look again at the actions of Judas and Christian views of him on pages 70–71.

Activities

3   **Hot-seat activity – interview with Judas**
    Imagine that you are Judas and have been asked to appear on a television programme about Jesus' last week before the crucifixion. Imagine your feelings and how you could describe them to others. (You could include Peter in the hot-seat to share the questions.)

Summary

The religious authorities plotted to kill Jesus, helped by the disciple Judas. At the Last Supper, Jesus predicted that he would be betrayed by a disciple.

exam zone

KnowZone
Conflict and argument

Quick quiz

1 What is 'corban'?

2 Who were the Pharisees?

3 On what day is the Jewish Sabbath?

4 Who were the scribes?

5 What usually happened at the Temple?

6 Who are sinners?

7 What is ritual cleanliness?

8 What happened on the first Palm Sunday?

9 What is the Law?

10 Who were the Sadducees?

Find out more

The following books are good places to find out more:

- *Mark's gospel – An Interpretation for Today* by Robin Cooper (Hodder, ISBN 0-340-43029-X)

- *Mark: A Gospel for Today* 3rd ed by Simon and Christopher Danes (St Mark's Press, ISBN 9-781-9070-6200-1)

- *Revise GCSE Religious Studies* (Letts, ISBN-13 9-781-8431-5515-7)

You can also find out more in the Christianity section of the BBC's Religion website. Go to www.pearsonschoolsandfecolleges.co.uk/hotlinks (express code 4271P) and click on the appropriate link.

Student tips

I found it really useful to make learning posters with plenty of colour, symbols and drawings to highlight the key points and the topics. I pinned them up somewhere I could see them regularly to keep reminding me. This really helped in answering the third question in the exam, where you have to explain things clearly.

Plenary activity

Design an ideas map of all the different topics in this section on conflict and argument. The one here has been started to give you some help.

Conflict

Significance for Christians today

Jesus heals the paralysed man

The plot to kill Jesus

Anointing at Bethany

Argument with the Sadducees

Disagreements about the Sabbath

Conflict and argument

Caesar and taxes

Disagreements about the meaning of the law

Jesus' predictions of the Passion

Jesus' entry into Jerusalem

Jesus cleanses the Temple

Argument about authority

Self-evaluation checklist

How well have you understood the topics in this section? In the first column of the table below use the following code to rate your understanding:

Green – I understand this fully.

Orange – I am confident I can answer most questions on this.

Red – I need to do a lot more work on this topic.

In the second and third columns you need to think about:

- whether you have an opinion on this topic and could give reasons for that opinion if asked
- whether you can give the opinion of someone who disagrees with you and give reasons for this alternative opinion.

Content covered	My understanding is red/orange/green	Can I give my opinion?	Can I give an alternative opinion?
Why the healing of the paralysed man led to conflict			
Its significance for Christians today			
Why disagreements about the Sabbath led to conflict			
Their significance for Christians today, particularly in relation to current issues of social and community cohesion			
Why disagreements about the meaning of the Law led to conflict			
Their significance for Christians today, particularly in relation to current issues of social and community cohesion			
Why Jesus' predictions of his Passion might have led to conflict			
Their significance for Christians today			
Why Jesus' entry into Jerusalem might have caused conflict			
Its significance for Christians today			
Why Jesus' cleansing of the Temple might have caused conflict			
The significance of this for Christians today, particularly in relation to current issues of social and community cohesion			
Why the argument about authority might have led to conflict			
Its significance for Christians today			
Why Jesus' answer to the question about Caesar and taxes might have led to conflict			
The significance of this for Christians today, particularly in relation to current issues of social and community cohesion			
Why Jesus' argument with the Sadducees about resurrection might have led to conflict			
Its significance for Christians today			
Why the anointing at Bethany might have led to conflict			
Its significance for Christians today			
The meaning and significance of the plot to kill Jesus			

KnowZone
Conflict and argument

Introduction

In the exam you will see a choice of two questions on this section. Each question will include four tasks that test your knowledge, understanding and evaluation of the material covered. A 2-mark question will ask you to define a term; a 4-mark question will ask you to give your opinion on a point of view; an 8-mark question will ask you to explain a particular belief or idea; a 6-mark question will ask for your opinion on a point of view and ask you to consider an alternative point of view.

Here you need to give a short accurate definition. You do not need to write more than one clear sentence.

The important words in the question are 'explain why', so you must make sure that this is what you focus on in your answer. This is worth 8 marks, so you must be prepared to spend some time answering it. You will also be assessed on your use of language in this question.

As before, give reasons you have learned in class. You must show you understand why people have these other views, even if you don't agree with them.

Mini exam paper

(a) What is the **Sabbath**?
   (2 marks)

(b) Do you think Jesus was right to cleanse the Temple?
   Give **two** reasons for your point of view. (4 marks)

(c) Explain why Jesus' argument with the Sadducees about resurrection is important for Christians today. (8 marks)

(d) 'Christians should avoid conflict with the authorities.'
   In your answer you should refer to Mark's gospel and Christianity.
   (i) Do you agree? Give reasons for your opinion. (3 marks)
   (ii) Give reasons why some people may disagree with you. (3 marks)

You must give your opinion but make sure you do give two clear and properly thought-out reasons. These can be ones you have learned in class.

In your answer you should state whether you agree or disagree with the statement, and you need to support your opinion with reasons.

Mark scheme

(a) You can earn **2 marks** for a correct answer, and **1 mark** for a partially correct answer.

(b) To earn up to the full **4 marks** you need to give two reasons and develop them. Two brief reasons or only one developed reason will earn **2 marks**.

(c) You can earn **7–8 marks** by giving up to four reasons, but the fewer reasons you give, the more you must develop them. Because you are being assessed on use of language, you also need to take care to express your understanding in a clear style of English and make some use of specialist vocabulary.

(d) To go beyond **3 marks** for the whole of this question you must refer to Christianity and Mark's gospel. The more you are able to develop your reasons, the more marks you will earn. Three simple reasons can earn you the same mark as one fully developed reason.

ResultsPlus
Build Better Answers

(d) 'Christians should avoid conflict with the authorities.'
In your answer you should refer to Mark's gospel and Christianity.
(i) Do you agree? Give reasons for your opinion. (3 marks)
(ii) Give reasons why some people may disagree with you. (3 marks)

Student answer	Comments	Improved student answer
(i) I disagree with the statement, Jesus was in conflict with the authorities when he argued with them about the Sabbath laws. He told them that the Sabbath was made for man, and not man for the Sabbath, so that people did not have to obey every rule set by those authorities.	In (i) the student has started by saying whether they agree with the statement, and then given a single developed reason, so would gain 2 marks. Two developed reasons, three simple reasons, or a fully developed reason would be needed to get full marks.	(i) I disagree with the statement, because Jesus was in conflict with the authorities when he argued with them about the Sabbath laws. He told them that the Sabbath was made for man, and not man for the Sabbath, so that people did not have to obey every rule set by those authorities. Jesus had other conflicts with the authorities over eating with tax collectors and sinners. He also cleansed the Temple in his argument with them over their allowing trading to take place.
(ii) However, because some Christians believe that what Jesus said in Mark about giving to Caesar what is Caesar's means they should not cause trouble with the authorities. Some Christian churches teach that Christians should obey those in charge.	In (ii) the student has given two simple reasons, without development, so would only receive 2 marks for this. If there were another simple reason given, or if these two were developed, the full 3 marks could be gained. The answer has been taken from both Mark's gospel and Christianity, as the question requires.	(ii) However, some Christians believe that what Jesus said in Mark about giving to Caesar what is Caesar's means they should not cause trouble with the authorities. Jesus himself never became directly involved in resisting the authorities, even asking why they came to arrest him with armed guards. He asked, 'Am I leading a rebellion?' Some Christian churches teach that Christians should obey those in charge. They believe that the gospel is primarily concerned with the spiritual, so they should not interfere and should allow the civil authorities to make the political decisions.

Death and resurrection

Introduction

The purpose of this section is to help you explore and think about the events that led up to the death of Jesus and his subsequent resurrection. These events have been key parts of the Christian faith ever since and, in many ways, they set Christianity apart from other religions. All sorts of issues are raised; all sorts of questions arise.

Learning outcomes for this section

By the end of this section, you should be able to:

- give definitions of the key words and use them in answers to GCSE questions
- explain the meaning and significance of the Last Supper for Mark
- explain why the Last Supper is important for Christians today
- explain the meaning and significance of the prayers in Gethsemane and why they might cause problems for some Christians today
- explain the meaning and significance of the betrayal and arrest in Mark and why there are different attitudes to Judas among Christians today
- explain the meaning and significance of the trial before the High Priest in Mark and how it affects Christian attitudes to justice
- explain the meaning and significance of the trial before Pilate in Mark and why Christians today see its significance differently from Mark
- explain the meaning and significance of the crucifixion in Mark
- explain why the crucifixion is important for Christians today
- explain the meaning and significance of burial for Christians today
- explain the meaning and significance of the resurrection for Mark as recorded in 16:1–8
- explain the meaning and significance of the resurrection for Christians today.

edexcel ▦ key terms

blasphemy	Gethsemane	Judas Iscariot	Pontius Pilate
crucifixion	Golgotha	Last Supper	Sanhedrin
Feast of Unleavened Bread	High Priest	Passover	upper room

The painting of the crucifixion above is by Andrea Mantegna, who lived between 1431 and 1506. Compare it to the modern portrayal (left), a still from the film *The Passion of the Christ* (2004).

- Which do you think is the more realistic?
- Working with a partner, write down any features you can remember from the story of the crucifixion.
- Now share your list with another pair. Have you been able to provide much of the story?
- In your exercise book, use a double-page spread. Copy the table shown on the right. On the left-hand page, write 'The Death of Jesus' and on the right-hand page write 'The Resurrection of Jesus'.

The Death of Jesus	The Resurrection of Jesus

Fill in any details which you already know about what Christians believe about the death and resurrection of Jesus. As the lessons continue, come back to this table and add more details.

3.1 The meaning and significance of the Last Supper for Mark (1)

The story of the **Last Supper**, which we will be looking at over the next four pages, is best considered in three sections:

• the preparation for **Passover**

• the supper itself

• Jesus' warning of Peter's denial.

Activities

1 Have you ever had to get your house ready for a big party – perhaps, for someone's birthday?

• Working in pairs, consider what preparations you would need to make? Write them down in a list.

• Now imagine that you are asked to go into town to prepare a room for that special meal.

Write down the other preparations that would be necessary.

edexcel ⠿ key terms

Feast of Unleavened Bread – The first day of the Passover festival.

Last Supper – The last meal Jesus ate with his disciples, which founded the Eucharist.

Passover – Jewish festival celebrating the release from Egypt.

upper room – The place where the Last Supper took place.

The preparation for Passover

It was Thursday – the day of the **Feast of Unleavened Bread** – the first day of the Jewish Passover celebrations. The disciples are sent by Jesus to prepare the room in Jerusalem for the evening meal:

'On the first day of the Feast of Unleavened Bread, when it was customary to sacrifice the Passover lamb, Jesus' disciples asked him, "Where do you want us to go and make preparations for you to eat the Passover?" So he sent two of his disciples, telling them, "Go into the city, and a man carrying a jar of water will meet you. Follow him. Say to the owner of the house he enters, 'The Teacher asks: Where is my guest room, where I may eat the Passover with my disciples?' He will show you a large **upper room**, furnished and ready. Make preparations for us there." The disciples left, went into the city and found things just as Jesus had told them. So they prepared the Passover.'
(Mark 14:12–16)

ResultsPlus
Build Better Answers

What was the **upper room**? (2 marks)

● **Good, 1-mark answers**
This will give a partly correct answer.

⚠ **Excellent, 2-mark answers**
These will give a short, accurate description.

As part of their preparations, the two disciples may have gone to the Temple to fetch the Passover lamb, which had to be killed as a sacrifice. Priests at the Temple would perform the sacrifice. The blood of the lamb would be thrown on the altar by the priests and then the carcass could be taken back for the meal later in the evening. This was symbolic of the original Passover, when the Jews escaped from Egypt. Then they had daubed the blood of a lamb above their doors and on the doorposts of their homes so that the Angel of Death would pass over them and only kill the firstborn of the Egyptians (see Exodus 12:21–28).

In this passage, Jesus' authority is again seen clearly. Just as when he sent the disciples to fetch a colt for his entry into Jerusalem, in the same way here the two disciples sent to make arrangements for the Passover celebration find everything just as Jesus had said.

The Last Supper

'When evening came, Jesus arrived with the Twelve. While they were reclining at the table eating, he said, "I tell you the truth, one of you will betray me – one who is eating with me." They were saddened, and one by one they said to him, "Surely not I?" "It is one of the Twelve," he replied, "one who dips bread into the bowl with me. The Son of Man will go just as it is written about him. But woe to that man who betrays the Son of Man! It would be better for him if he had not been born." While they were eating, Jesus took bread, gave thanks and broke it, and gave it to his disciples, saying, "Take it; this is my body." Then he took the cup, gave thanks and offered it to them, and they all drank from it. This is my blood of the covenant, which is poured out for many," he said to them. "I tell you the truth, I will not drink again of the fruit of the vine until that day when I drink it anew in the kingdom of God." When they had sung a hymn, they went out to the Mount of Olives.' (Mark 14:17–26)

A painting of the Last Supper by the 16th-century Italian painter Jacopo Bassano.

3.1 The meaning and significance of the Last Supper for Mark (2)

How does the Last Supper compare to a Jewish Passover meal?

While some scholars have suggested that it could not have been a Passover meal because the Jewish Law would not allow a trial or an execution on a feast day, Mark is at pains to say it was. In support of this, there was a dispute at the time between the Pharisees and Sadducees as to the start of the festival. The Pharisees had decided to take the meal on the day before the official date, so Jesus would be following their custom, in this case by celebrating Passover on the Thursday evening.

Leonardo da Vinci's painting of the Last Supper is one of the most famous images in the world. Why would he – and so many other artists – have wanted to paint this event?

Jewish Seder plate used during the Passover meal.

The links with the Passover are:

- Jesus describes the bowl in which the disciples dip their bread (Mark 14:20) – possibly used for the bitter herbs in the Passover meal
- the words he speaks over the bread and wine have parallels with the words spoken by the head of the family to explain the significance of the food and drink in the Passover meal (Mark 14:22–25)
- the Passover instructions required the use of red wine and Jesus links this to his blood, due to be shed at the crucifixion (Mark 14:24)
- finally, before they leave for the Mount of Olives, they sing hymns, and this was another part of the Passover instructions (Mark 14:26).

Significance for Mark

Mark wants his readers to make the connection between the Last Supper and Passover. In much the same way that the Passover was a turning point in the Jewish faith, in which the Jews were liberated from slavery in Egypt, so now Jesus' ministry on Earth was reaching its turning point – he would liberate his followers and restore their relationship with God.

Mark also feels that the Last Supper is important because it was the last time that Jesus was with his disciples before his betrayal and death. He wanted the followers of Jesus to understand the significance of the bread broken – that it represents his body broken on the cross – and the wine – representing his shed blood. He was writing for Christians who were being persecuted, tortured and killed for their faith. Many may have wondered what God was doing to allow his people to suffer like this. Mark links Jesus very clearly to the Passover story of the escape of the Jews from Egypt as recorded in the

book of Exodus. God's deliverance of his chosen people from slavery was now Jesus' deliverance of his people from sin.

Activities

3　The Romans persecuted the early Christians because they claimed the faith was cannibalistic – they were eating Jesus' body and blood. How do you think this claim originated?

4　At the time, Christianity was still viewed as a sect of the Jewish faith. What evidence do you see for this?

Jesus' warning of Peter's denial

'"You will all fall away," Jesus told them, "for it is written: 'I will strike the shepherd, and the sheep will be scattered.' But after I have risen, I will go ahead of you into Galilee." Peter declared, "Even if all fall away, I will not."

'"I tell you the truth," Jesus answered, "today – yes, tonight – before the rooster crows twice you yourself will disown me three times." But Peter insisted emphatically, "Even if I have to die with you, I will never disown you." And all the others said the same.' (Mark 14:27–31)

You will have read about Peter's denial in the discipleship section, but it is important here because Jesus predicted Peter's – and the other disciples' – failure and they could not believe it. Within hours they had all deserted him and Peter was swearing that he did not know Jesus.

Activities

5　What other prediction does Jesus make? (Clue: look up Mark 16:7.)

6　Why do you think Mark includes this?

Summary

The Last Supper was an important part of Jesus' story as it linked Jesus to the Jewish Passover. At the meal, he took bread and wine in the Jewish tradition but then gave it a new meaning and significance.

3.2 Why the Last Supper is important for Christians today

66

St Paul is responsible for much of the teaching in the Christian Church, and it is in his First Letter to the Corinthians that he explains why the Last Supper is important to Christians. Read this extract and see whether you can find the answer for yourself:

'For I received from the Lord what I also passed on to you: The Lord Jesus, on the night he was betrayed, took bread, and when he had given thanks, he broke it and said, "This is my body, which is for you; do this in remembrance of me." In the same way, after supper he took the cup, saying, "This cup is the new covenant in my blood; do this, whenever you drink it, in remembrance of me." For whenever you eat this bread and drink this cup, you proclaim the Lord's death until he comes.'
(1 Corinthians 11:23–26)

Activities

1 After reading this passage, why do you think the Last Supper is important for Christians today?

The Last Supper for today's Christians

Christians today take the Last Supper as the basis for a service of celebration – the Eucharist. In different denominations it has different titles and different emphases. The Roman Catholic, Eastern Orthodox and some Anglican (Anglo-Catholic) Churches broadly share the following beliefs:

Mass, Liturgy or Eucharist
• The whole service is a celebration of the sacrifice made by Jesus.
• The body and blood of Jesus are being brought before the people afresh in the bread and the wine received.
• When people receive the bread and wine they believe that they are really receiving the actual body and blood of Jesus. (This is the doctrine called 'transubstantiation'.)

There are three different views within the Protestant tradition all dating back to the 16th century when the Reformation began, where three of the major reformers questioned the teachings of the Roman Catholic Church.

Martin Luthur's view	John Calvin's view	Zwingli's view
• Jesus is really present in, with, and beneath the bread and wine offered in the celebration.	• Jesus is really present in the bread and the wine in a spiritual way, as they are consumed.	• The bread and wine are no more than symbols, intended to remind believers of Jesus' death and resurrection.
• There is no real change in the bread or wine.	• But, again, there is no suggestion of change.	• Evangelical Christians and most nonconformist Churches hold to this view.
• The Lutheran Church and some members of the Church of England hold to this view.	• The broad stream of the Church of England holds to this view.	

The Eucharist is an important part of Church services for many Christians.

Others, such as the Religious Society of Friends (Quakers) and the Salvation Army, do not celebrate the Eucharist as they feel it is very important for Christians not to rely on the outward trappings of worship.

Most Christians, however, agree on how important the service is, for they share the basic beliefs that:

- Jesus began this meal at the Last Supper
- he is present as the Church meets to celebrate and is received by faith
- the service is intended to remind Christians of Jesus' death and resurrection
- it enables Christians to 'commune' with Jesus and each other
- through the service, the Church can look forward to Jesus' return to Earth and his establishment of the kingdom of God on Earth.

For discussion

Do you think it should be important for all Christians to believe exactly the same about this service, or does it not matter?

Summary

The celebration of the Last Supper has become the most important ceremony to be held by many Christian denominations. Different groups have differing views on the actual meaning of the ceremony, however.

Activities

2 A television company is producing a programme comparing the celebration of the Last Supper in different Churches. In small groups you are to prepare a five-minute part of the programme to explain one Church's way of celebrating the Eucharist.

3.3 Jesus' prayers in the Garden of Gethsemane

Learning outcomes

By the end of this lesson, you should be able to:

● state the meaning of the prayers in Gethsemane

● give your own opinion, with a reason, about why Jesus prayed here

● explain why Gethsemane is an important place to Christians

● evaluate different points of view about why this might cause problems for Christians today.

edexcel ::: key terms

Gethsemane – The place where Jesus was arrested.

Activities

1 Do you have a place where you go when you just want to relax? Describe it to a partner. What are its main features?

Crisis in Gethsemane

Agony in the Garden (c1460) by Andrea Mantegna. Pick out the main features of this painting and explain what the artist is trying to say about this event.

In Section 1, on discipleship, this story was featured as an example of the disciples' failure to always follow Jesus' commands (see pages 22–23). Now we focus on Jesus himself in the Garden of Gethsemane. What was going through his mind as he brought the Twelve there initially, and then took three of them – Peter, James and John – further into the garden with him?

'They went to a place called Gethsemane, and Jesus said to his disciples, "Sit here while I pray." He took Peter, James and John along with him, and he began to be deeply distressed and troubled. "My soul is overwhelmed with sorrow to the point of death," he said to them. "Stay here and keep watch."

'Going a little farther, he fell to the ground and prayed that if possible the hour might pass from him. "Abba, Father," he said, "everything is possible for you. Take this cup from me. Yet not what I will, but what you will." Then he returned to his disciples and found them sleeping. "Simon," he said to Peter, "are you asleep? Could you not keep watch for one hour? Watch and pray so that you will not fall into temptation. The spirit is willing, but the body is weak." Once more he went away and prayed the same thing. When he came back, he again found them sleeping, because their eyes were heavy. They did not know what to say to him. Returning the third time, he said to them, "Are you still sleeping and resting? Enough! The hour has come. Look, the Son of Man is betrayed into the hands of sinners. Rise! Let us go! Here comes my betrayer!"' (Mark 14:32–42)

This section is important, for it shows both Jesus' humanity and his divinity. As God, Jesus knew that death awaited him. As a human, he anticipated the torture he would have to face at the hands of Roman guards before he was killed. He had to go through human agonies of despair, fear, tiredness and even trying to avoid the suffering if possible. At the same time, as he prayed, he said 'Abba' – the Aramaic word for 'father'. He appealed for help from God, his Father. In Jesus' time, most Jewish people would have thought this a disrespectful way to talk to God, but Mark recognised how close Jesus was to God, so that it would be completely appropriate. Gethsemane became the place where Jesus accepted that his mission to the world involved suffering and death.

The depression, even desperation, of Jesus turned to disappointment as he returned to find the disciples fast asleep. As if that were not bad enough, he went away and returned twice more, but the same thing happened each time. This failure of the disciples to support him must have been crushing, yet Jesus knew that he had to carry on. He recognised that they would let him down if they could not even stay awake and pray: they might want to help, but they were weak. That was why he said, 'Watch and pray so that you will not fall into temptation. The spirit is willing, but the body is weak' (Mark 13:38). Christians need to pray for the strength to stay faithful.

Activities

2   Analyse the passage carefully. Pick out the parts that show the divine side of Jesus. Pick out the parts that show the humanity of Jesus. Are there any that show both?

Why might this passage cause problems for Christians today?

How could God the Son be 'deeply distressed and troubled' – surely Jesus should not feel this way?

Why would Jesus ask God to take this cup away from him? Did he not trust his father, God?

If he had to ask questions of God anyway, perhaps Jesus is not God?

The disciples fall asleep when Jesus needs them most. Not very promising for people like Peter – the first Pope!

Jesus said, 'Not what I will, but what you will' – doesn't this suggest that Jesus was separate from God rather than part of the Trinity?

Activities

3   Above are some people's ideas about the problems with this passage in Mark. Go through each one – what do you think? How do you think a Christian might reply to these issues?

Summary

In this lesson you have looked at the background to Jesus praying in the Garden of Gethsemane, just before his arrest. Both Jesus' humanity and his divinity are shown. Christians today may have problems with this as it shows Jesus' weakness – how could God be weak?

3.4 Betrayal and arrest

Learning outcomes

By the end of this lesson, you should be able to:

● state the meaning of the betrayal and arrest of Jesus in Gethsemane

● give your own opinion, with a reason, about why Jesus was betrayed here

● explain why the arrest is an important event to Christians

● evaluate different attitudes towards Judas among Christians today.

The meaning and importance of Jesus' betrayal and arrest

'Just as he [Jesus] was speaking, Judas, one of the Twelve, appeared. With him was a crowd armed with swords and clubs, sent from the chief priests, the teachers of the law, and the elders. Now the betrayer had arranged a signal with them: "The one I kiss is the man; arrest him and lead him away under guard." Going at once to Jesus, Judas said, "Rabbi!" and kissed him. The men seized Jesus and arrested him. Then one of those standing near drew his sword and struck the servant of the high priest, cutting off his ear. "Am I leading a rebellion," said Jesus, "that you have come out with swords and clubs to capture me? Every day I was with you, teaching in the temple courts, and you did not arrest me. But the Scriptures must be fulfilled." Then everyone deserted him and fled. A young man, wearing nothing but a linen garment, was following Jesus. When they seized him, he fled naked, leaving his garment behind.'
(Mark 14:43–52)

The High Priest's men needed **Judas Iscariot**'s help to find Jesus away from the public gaze (see pages 54–55). In Mark's description, Judas comes with 'a crowd armed with swords and clubs', which shows they were worried that Jesus and his followers might resist arrest. Perhaps this shows that they

edexcel ::: key terms

Judas Iscariot – The disciple who betrayed Jesus.

were expecting Jesus to be the warrior-like Messiah that many people expected. Maybe they were right to come in force, however, as one of Jesus' disciples draws his sword, slicing a man's ear. In Luke's gospel, Jesus heals him.

However, it was a group sent by the Jewish leaders who came for Jesus, not Roman soldiers. Although the Jews could try Jesus in a religious court, they had to go to the Romans for a penalty to be imposed.

For Christians, the betrayal and arrest of Jesus shows how his life continues to fulfil the Old Testament prophecies: 'But the Scriptures must be fulfilled'. It also shows that the disciples were only human beings and were scared and ran away. This should encourage Christians when they find the teachings of Jesus difficult to follow and fail to live up to their own expectations.

Activities

1 How does Jesus explain why his arrest happens in this way?

2 Re-tell the story of Jesus' arrest and betrayal. You could present this as a cartoon with speech bubbles or as a written account.

Mark's view of Judas

When Mark first mentions Judas (Mark 3:19) he says: '... and Judas Iscariot, who betrayed Jesus'. Therefore, Judas is presented as the 'traitor' figure from the start. Mark presents the moment of betrayal very memorably – a kiss should be an innocent gesture, as would the greeting, 'Rabbi'. Does this make the betrayal seem worse? Mark clearly felt that this was the ultimate betrayal. In Matthew's gospel, Judas commits suicide afterwards, which suggests that he was sorry for what he had done.

Attitudes to Judas among Christians today

Most Christians consider Judas a traitor, because Jesus said he would be betrayed. The word 'Judas' is now used to mean 'betrayer'. However, it could be argued that Judas had no choice. He had to fulfil his destiny – and Jesus' destiny too. At the Last Supper, Jesus told his disciples that one would betray him, but he did not try to stop it. This may suggest that Judas existed only to betray Jesus and fulfil the prophecy.

Kiss of Judas Iscariot, *anonymous 12th-century painting, Uffizi Gallery, Florence.*

Judas betrays Jesus with a Kiss *(1602) by Caravaggio.*

Because of this, some Christians today view Judas differently from the way he appears in Mark's gospel. They think there might be several possible explanations for Judas' actions:

- Perhaps Judas himself had been arrested when Jesus cleansed the Temple and in return for freedom he agreed to hand over Jesus.
- Was Judas disillusioned when he realised that Jesus had no intention of becoming a political or military Messiah, or did he want to force Jesus' hand, thinking his arrest would lead to an uprising against Roman rule?
- Or what if the betrayal was a deliberate act towards fulfilling prophecy? If so, Judas might have acted with Jesus' full agreement in 'betraying' his master.
- Another alternative is that Judas' motivation in betraying Jesus to the Romans was to help him. As a close friend, Judas was helping Jesus to fulfil his destiny to die on the cross. Judas would be the catalyst for what would become the salvation of humanity.

Activities

3 What are your own opinions of Judas? Do you see him as a 'traitor'? Explain why or why not. Then explain why some people may disagree with you.

Challenge

4 Look at these two paintings and the one on page 55 for different perspectives on the same subject from artists from the 12th to the 17th centuries.

- What image of Judas do you see in each of them? Do the images change with time?
- How might an artist portray this story in the 21st century?

Summary

Jesus was betrayed by one of his close friends and arrested. Mark views Judas as the ultimate betrayer, but some Christians today have different attitudes towards him.

3.5 Trial before the High Priest

Learning outcomes

By the end of this lesson, you should be able to:

● describe the trial before the High Priest

● give your own opinion, with a reason, about why Jesus was tried before the High Priest

● explain why this trial had to take place

● evaluate different points of view about why this might affect Christian attitudes to justice today.

edexcel ⠿ key terms

blasphemy – Associating oneself with God / language or deeds that insult God.

High Priest – The chief Jewish leader at the time of Jesus.

Sanhedrin – The supreme Jewish council which found Jesus guilty of blasphemy.

The **Sanhedrin**, led by the **High Priest**, was the highest Jewish court, responsible for trying all criminal cases, as well as dealing with religious issues. Its powers were limited, however, because the Roman occupiers had ultimate power.

The Jewish Law – the Torah – says:

'One witness is not enough to convict a man accused of any crime or offence he may have committed. A matter must be established by the testimony of two or three witnesses. If a malicious witness takes the stand to accuse a man of a crime, the two men involved in the dispute must stand in the presence of the LORD before the priests and the judges who are in office at the time. The judges must make a thorough investigation, and if the witness proves to be a liar, giving false testimony against his brother, then do to him as he intended to do to his brother.' (Deuteronomy 19:15–19b)

This means that two witnesses can provide conclusive proof, but one witness cannot. However, the testimony of one witness can at least require a defendant to swear to his innocence or guilt.

Jesus brought to trial

'They took Jesus to the high priest, and all the chief priests, elders and teachers of the law came together. Peter followed him at a distance, right into the courtyard of the high priest. There he sat with the guards and warmed himself at the fire. The chief priests and the whole Sanhedrin were looking for evidence against Jesus so that they could put him to death, but they did not find any. Many testified falsely against him, but their statements did not agree. Then some stood up and gave this false testimony against him: "We heard him say, 'I will destroy this man-made temple and in three days will build another, not made by man.'" Yet even then their testimony did not agree. Then the high priest stood up before them and asked Jesus, "Are you not going to answer? What is this testimony that these men are bringing against you?" But Jesus remained silent and gave no answer. Again the high priest asked him, "Are you the Christ, the Son of the Blessed One?" "I am," said Jesus. "And you will see the Son of Man sitting at the right hand of the Mighty One and coming on the clouds of heaven." The high priest tore his clothes. "Why do we need any more witnesses?" he asked. "You have heard the **blasphemy**. What do you think?" They all condemned him as worthy of death. Then some began to spit at him; they blindfolded him, struck him with their fists, and said, "Prophesy!" And the guards took him and beat him.' (Mark 14:53–65)

Activities

1 Describe, in your own words, the trial before the High Priest.

2 What were the false witnesses claiming Jesus had said?

3 How does this trial fit with the requirements of the Torah for witnesses to agree?

Trials involving a death sentence were not allowed at night, and a guilty verdict had to be delayed 24 hours before sentence was carried out by the Romans, who also had to agree with the punishment. False witnesses would suffer the same fate as the accused. Beating a prisoner during the court hearing would have been unacceptable.

Some people think this trial was merely a preparation for the 'proper' trial before Pontius Pilate, the Roman governor. Mark says Jesus remained silent throughout, and it seems that they struggled to find evidence to convict him. In the end, Jesus condemns himself when he acknowledges, in public for the first time, that he is the Christ, the Messiah. Obviously this makes the statement especially important for Mark.

The High Priest tore Jesus' robe as a symbol to show blasphemy had been committed. In claiming to be the Christ, Jesus associated himself with God and deserved to die. The Roman authorities alone could impose the death penalty, so the Sanhedrin needed to convince Pilate that the death penalty was required.

How might this trial affect Christian attitudes towards justice today?

The trial was unusual, and most people today would probably say that justice was not done. It is clear that the Sanhedrin did not follow the rules found in the passage from Deuteronomy. This event might then encourage Christians to be sure that justice is not only done but is also seen to be done. They might also think that the law must always be followed properly and cannot be allowed to be influenced by personal feelings or animosity, as it was here.

The Old Bailey is the most important court of law in the UK today. On top of the building is a statue of Lady Justice. Do you think that Jesus' trial before the High Priest was just?

Activities

4 How might this story of an unjust and unfair trial be an encouragement to Christians undergoing persecution?

5 How might this affect Christian attitudes to justice today? Give different points of view in your answer.

Summary

Jesus was put on trial before the Jewish authorities, but the rules from the Jewish Law were not followed. Jesus answered that he was the Christ and was condemned and beaten. This trial might affect Christian views on justice today.

3.6 Trial before Pontius Pilate

Learning outcomes

By the end of this lesson, you should be able to:

● explain the meaning of the trial before Pontius Pilate

● evaluate different points of view about why this trial might be viewed differently today as compared with Mark's view.

edexcel ⠿ key terms

Pontius Pilate – The Roman procurator (governor) of Judea at the time of Jesus.

The trial

'Very early in the morning, the chief priests, with the elders, the teachers of the law and the whole Sanhedrin, reached a decision. They bound Jesus, led him away and handed him over to Pilate.

'"Are you the king of the Jews?" asked Pilate. "Yes, it is as you say," Jesus replied. The chief priests accused him of many things. So again Pilate asked him, "Aren't you going to answer? See how many things they are accusing you of." But Jesus still made no reply, and Pilate was amazed.

'Now it was the custom at the Feast to release a prisoner whom the people requested. A man called Barabbas was in prison with the insurrectionists who had committed murder in the uprising. The crowd came up and asked Pilate to do for them what he usually did. "Do you want me to release to you the king of the Jews?" asked Pilate, knowing it was out of envy that the chief priests had handed Jesus over to him. But the chief priests stirred up the crowd to have Pilate release Barabbas instead. "What shall I do, then, with the one you call the king of the Jews?" Pilate asked them.

'"Crucify him!" they shouted. "Why? What crime has he committed?" asked Pilate. But they shouted all the louder, "Crucify him!" Wanting to satisfy the crowd, Pilate released Barabbas to them. He had Jesus flogged, and handed him over to be crucified.'

(Mark 15:1–15)

Antonio Ciseri's depiction of Pontius Pilate presenting a scourged Christ to the people, Ecce homo! (Behold the man!), was painted in the 19th century.

Who was Pilate?

Pontius Pilate was the Roman prefect, the governor of the province of Judea between 26 and 36 CE. One contemporary historian, Philo, described him as a violent thug, fond of executions without trial. Another, Josephus, records that, at the start of his term, Pilate provoked the Jews by ordering the imperial standards (banners) to be carried into Jerusalem. He later helped himself to Jewish revenues to build an aqueduct and sent in soldiers who killed hundreds of people protesting against the project. This was the man who had the power to decide whether Jesus lived or died.

Activities

1 From the description above and the painting opposite, what sort of man do you think Pilate was?

2 Now read Mark's account of the trial – are you surprised by Pilate's behaviour?

Mark's portrayal of Jesus' trial in front of Pilate has several features that would have been important at the time of writing:

- Jesus' behaviour – throughout both of the trials, Jesus says very little and does not try to defend himself. Mark's description ties in with the prediction of the scripture written several hundred years before Jesus, which Christians would have known:

> 'He was oppressed and afflicted, yet he did not open his mouth; he was led like a lamb to the slaughter, and as a sheep before her shearers is silent, so he did not open his mouth. By oppression and judgment he was taken away.' (Isaiah 53:7–8)

- Pilate's behaviour – as with all the gospel writers, Mark shows Pilate as reluctant to condemn Jesus. He even offers to free Jesus, but the crowd chooses to release Barabbas (who had led a minor revolt against the Romans).
- The behaviour of the crowd – Mark seems intent on blaming the crucifixion of Jesus on the Jewish crowd who were stirred up by the chief priests. Pilate seems to fear the crowd – he could not be sure that releasing Jesus might not cause a riot,

and above everything else Pilate needed to keep order or he might have lost his job. By the time the gospel was written, Pilate had, in fact, been recalled to Rome because of a riot.

Activities

3 Write a report of the trial that includes an explanation of:
- why Jesus was tried by the Roman governor
- what Jesus was accused of
- why you think Pilate wanted to release Jesus
- why he did not release him.

How today's Christians view the trial

Many Christians in the past blamed Jewish people for the death of Jesus because of the accounts in the gospels. This led to hundreds of years of anti-Semitism and persecution of Jewish people by Christians. Today, most Christians see the trial as fulfilling God's plan.

Christians today realise that they should not be anti-Semitic because this goes against Jesus' teachings of treating everyone as you would wish to be treated, and also because Jesus himself was a Jew and lived according to Jewish Law.

In 2005 Pope Benedict XVI offered greetings to '... my brothers and sisters of the Jewish people, to whom we are joined by a great shared spiritual heritage, one rooted in God's irrevocable promises'.

Activities

4 Explain why many Christians today see the trial before Pilate differently from Christians in the past.

For discussion

Who is to blame for Jesus' death?

Summary

Jesus was sentenced to death by Pontius Pilate. Christians today view this trial differently from those of Mark's day.

3.7 The crucifixion according to Mark (1)

Learning outcomes

By the end of this lesson, you should be able to:

● describe the crucifixion of Jesus according to Mark

● give your own opinion, with a reason, about why Jesus was crucified

● explain why Jesus' death was important to Mark.

The Crucified Christ or The Yellow Christ (1889) by Paul Gaugin.

edexcel ⠿ key terms

crucifixion – The Roman death penalty suffered by Jesus when he was nailed to the cross.

Golgotha – The place of the skull; the place where Jesus was crucified.

Activities

1 Look up the Stations of the Cross on the Cumbria & Lancashire Education Online (CLEO) website by going to www.heinemann.co.uk/hotlinks (express code 4271P) and clicking on the appropriate link.

2 Many Christians retrace the journey of Jesus through Jerusalem to the spot where it is believed he was crucified. Why would they want to do this?

The importance of Jesus' crucifixion for Mark

Crucifixion was a punishment used only for slaves or major troublemakers, and Roman citizens were exempt from it. From the earliest accounts of crucifixion, it was thought to be the most painful form of death. To a Jew, it would seem even more horrible because of the curse that is written in Deuteronomy:

> '… you must not leave his body on the tree overnight. Be sure to bury him that same day, because anyone who is hung on a tree is under God's curse. You must not desecrate the land the LORD your God is giving you as an inheritance.'
> (Deuteronomy 21:23)

Mark does not make much of Jesus' physical suffering. The Romans crucified hundreds, if not thousands, of people, so for Mark it was more important to show his readers how Jesus bore the suffering. In that way, they would be helped to understand who Jesus was. The Old Testament prophecies told of the Suffering Servant of God (see page 113), and this was the message Mark wanted to convey to the early Christians as they faced persecution. If the founder of their faith could face suffering and rejection, then so could they.

> 'A certain man from Cyrene, Simon, the father of Alexander and Rufus, was passing by on his way in from the country, and they forced him to carry the cross. They brought Jesus to the place called **Golgotha** (which means The Place of the Skull). Then they offered him wine mixed with myrrh, but he did not take it. And they crucified him. Dividing up his clothes, they cast lots to see what each would get. It was the third hour when they crucified him. The written notice of the charge against him read: THE KING OF THE JEWS. They crucified two robbers with him, one on his right and one on his left. Those who passed by hurled insults at him, shaking their heads and saying, "So! You who are going to destroy the temple and build it in three days, come down from the cross and save yourself!" In the same way the chief priests and the teachers of the law mocked him among themselves. "He saved others," they said, "but he can't save himself! Let this Christ, this King of Israel, come down now from the cross, that we may see and believe." Those crucified with him also heaped insults on him.
>
> 'At the sixth hour darkness came over the whole land until the ninth hour. And at the ninth hour Jesus cried out in a loud voice, "Eloi, Eloi, lama sabachthani?" – which means, "My God, my God, why have you forsaken me?" When some of those standing near heard this, they said, "Listen, he's calling Elijah." One man ran, filled a sponge with wine vinegar, put it on a stick, and offered it to Jesus to drink. "Now leave him alone. Let's see if Elijah comes to take him down," he said. With a loud cry, Jesus breathed his last. The curtain of the temple was torn in two from top to bottom. And when the centurion, who stood there in front of Jesus, heard his cry and saw how he died, he said, "Surely this man was the Son of God!"' (Mark 15:21–39)

Let's break down the meaning and importance of each part of the story.

The road to Golgotha

- Simon of Cyrene only appears at this one point in Mark's gospel. His sons, Alexander and Rufus, became members of the Church (Romans 16:13), so it would seem that they could have been known to Mark's readers, possibly even fellow members of the Church in Rome. This would suggest Mark had an eyewitness to the event.
- At Golgotha, the drink offered to Jesus was a drug to help ease the extreme pain of the crucifixion, but Jesus refused it. He had to bear the full effect.
- The soldiers divided his clothes out by playing dice to see who would get each piece. This mirrors a verse from Psalm 22, a psalm that figures throughout Jesus' crucifixion: 'They divide my garments among them and cast lots for my clothing' (Psalm 22:18).

Activities

3 Look at the paintings of the crucifixion on pages 61 and 76–79. They are from a variety of different cultures.

- What do you think the artists are trying to portray about Jesus and his death?
- Why do you think artists from different countries would portray Jesus in these different ways?

The Crucifixion *by He Qi.*

3.7 The crucifixion according to Mark (2)

Jesus is crucified

- Jesus was nailed to the crossbeam by his wrists and then hoisted to the fixed upright of the cross. His feet were nailed to the upright. A small block of wood at the base of the spine would provide support for his body. Crucifixion was a slow process as the prisoner fought to lift his body to breathe and then dropped back to relieve the intense pain. As he weakened, he would slowly suffocate.

A 16th-century Russian byzantine painting of the crucifixion.

- The custom was to nail a written notice of what the person was guilty of above their head – in this case it read, 'The King of the Jews'. Pilate may have meant it to warn off other would-be revolutionaries, or maybe to insult the Jewish leaders. For Mark, it was important because it showed who Jesus really was. Israel may have rejected him, the Romans may not have recognised him, but here was the true King of Israel.

- Two robbers were crucified with him. Even at this stage, Jesus was to be found in the company of outcasts.

- Next came insults: if he was so powerful, why not save himself? How difficult would it be for him to come down from the cross? Psalm 22:8 talks of this deliverance. To Mark, the significance of this is that Jesus actually stayed on the cross because he was the Messiah. He could have saved himself, but the Messiah had to suffer and die in this way for a reason.

- 'At the sixth hour darkness came over the whole land until the ninth hour.' Was this a solar eclipse perhaps? Whatever it was, it lasted for three hours, from the sixth hour (12 noon) until the ninth hour (3 p.m.). Perhaps Mark was thinking of the prophecy in Amos 8:9b, 'I will make the sun go down at noon and darken the earth in broad daylight'? Darkness suggests that something terrible was happening. God was at work and in control, even as this act of great importance was unfolding.

- Mark wanted to show the importance of Jesus' suffering and death, and Jesus' words helped this too. Mark only records the words, '*Eloi, Eloi, lama sabachthani?*' – Aramaic for 'My God, my God, why have you forsaken me?' – the first line from Psalm 22. Was this a cry of despair as Jesus was about to die, deserted by his Father? Or did Jesus die before he could finish the Psalm?

- Some of the people watching thought Jesus was calling for Elijah the prophet. Traditionally, Elijah had been linked to the arrival of the Messiah, while some also believed he would come to help good people in trouble.

The death of Jesus

- As Jesus died, the Temple curtain was torn in two. He had taught that the Temple should be for all believers to meet with God, but the curtain had separated the 'Holy of Holies' from the rest. Only the High Priest could go into this section, under strict guidelines. The Holy of Holies had contained the Ark of the Covenant in the time of Solomon, but it was no longer there. Mark included this detail because the torn curtain symbolises the breakdown of the barrier separating people from God brought about by Jesus' death. The old, exclusive religion of the Jews is replaced by the inclusive gospel of Christianity.

- The Roman centurion summed up the events: 'Surely this man was the Son of God!' (Mark 15:39). Some people suggest that he was being sarcastic, but more likely he recognised Jesus as being the Messiah. The Romans would call their great heroes 'a son of God' or 'a son of the gods'. Mark would have included this to show that the first person to show faith in Jesus after his death was a Gentile. For Mark, as for the centurion and Christians ever since, Jesus was the Son of God who died on the cross.

The Crucifixion *by Peter Paul Rubens.*

Activities

4   Mark used several Old Testament references to underline the idea that Jesus was the Jewish Messiah. List the ways in which Mark shows links between Jesus and Old Testament prophecies.

5   Which parts of the story emphasise that Jesus is for all people, not just the Jews?

Challenge

6   Read Psalm 22 – how many references can you find that could be linked to Jesus' crucifixion?

Summary

Simon of Cyrene carried the cross for Jesus as he went to Golgotha, the place of crucifixion. Jesus suffered and died on the cross. Mark shows that Jesus' death is for Jews and Gentiles alike.

3.8 Why is the crucifixion important for Christians today?

So what does this mean to Christians today – why did Jesus have to die?

Christians have different views on Jesus' crucifixion.

Jesus' sacrifice

Many Christians view Jesus' death as the sacrifice to end all sacrifices because Jesus gives his blood voluntarily so that every person can bridge the gap between God and humanity. The diagrams below explain this idea.

In the 21st century some people may feel that this idea shows God as harsh and cruel in condemning his own son to suffering and death. Besides this, they reject the idea that God needed a perfect sacrifice. However, Jesus chose to be that sacrifice.

Christians believe that Jesus died to overcome the Original Sin that had separated people from God since the Garden of Eden. His sacrifice 'atoned' for the sins of humanity. This teaching is called the 'atonement'.

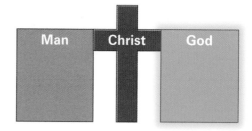

Christians believe Jesus was sent by God the Father to show people a way back to himself – to reconcile people to God.

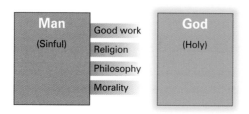

Many Christians believe that there is nothing they can do to get back in contact with God – no good works, no religion, no philosophy and no morality will bridge that gap.

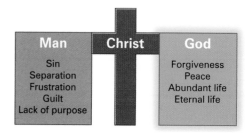

Some Christians believe that God was offended by the sins of the people so that Jesus' death was necessary to repay the debt. Jesus could repay this debt because he alone was perfect, and nothing less than perfection would satisfy God's sense of justice.

A ransom for many?

Other Christians think about this in a different way:

Mark wrote that Jesus gave 'his life as a ransom for many'. A ransom is a sum of money demanded for the release of somebody who is being held prisoner – a payment to ensure the release of the victim.

This ransom had to be paid to free people from their sin and bring them back to God.

God showed his love for humans to such an extent that he was prepared to allow Jesus to die on the cross as this ransom that would enable humanity to come back to him.

This view is explained by Paul who wrote:

'But God demonstrates his own love for us in this: While we were still sinners, Christ died for us.' (Romans 5:8)

Christians who do not agree with this view may ask why God would need a ransom to allow people to come back to him?

Activities

1 Look up Isaiah 53:7–8 and write these verses out. How do they seem to link to Jesus?

2 'If Jesus had not been crucified, there would have been no Christianity.'

Write down reasons why you might agree with this statement and then reasons why you might disagree. Having weighed up the arguments for and against, now explain whether you agree or whether you disagree.

ResultsPlus
Build Better Answers

Explain why the crucifixion is important to Christians today. (8 marks)

■ **Basic, 1–2-mark answers**
Answers which get low marks will give one simple reason.

● **Good, 3–6-mark answers**
Level 2 answers (3–4 marks) will give two brief reasons, or a developed reason. Level 3 answers (5–6 marks) will give three brief reasons, or a fully developed reason, or one simple reason and one developed reason.

▲ **Excellent, 7–8-mark answers**
Most excellent answers will show clear understanding of the issue by using four brief reasons, or two developed reasons, or two simple reasons and one developed reason, or a comprehensive explanation using one fully developed reason.

For discussion

In small groups, consider the two ways of looking at Jesus' death – as sacrifice or as ransom – why do you think Christians are divided in their understanding of the crucifixion?

Summary

Christians today have different understandings of the meaning and significance of the crucifixion. However, all believe that it was part of God's plan to enable humanity to return to him.

3.9 What is the meaning and significance of Jesus' burial?

Learning outcomes

By the end of this lesson, you should be able to:

● describe Jesus' burial

● give your own opinion, with a reason, about why Jesus was buried here

● explain why Jesus' burial place is important to Christians.

Jesus' burial

Leaving the bodies of those crucified on the crosses to rot and be eaten by birds was the normal practice as it would serve as a warning to others. It was unusual for crucified people to be buried, and Pilate himself would be the only one authorised to allow it:

> 'It was Preparation Day (that is, the day before the Sabbath). So as evening approached, Joseph of Arimathea, a prominent member of the Council, who was himself waiting for the kingdom of God, went boldly to Pilate and asked for Jesus' body. Pilate was surprised to hear that he was already dead. Summoning the centurion, he asked him if Jesus had already died. When he learned from the centurion that it was so, he gave the body to Joseph. So Joseph bought some linen cloth, took down the body, wrapped it in the linen, and placed it in a tomb cut out of rock. Then he rolled a stone against the entrance of the tomb. Mary Magdalene and Mary the mother of Jesus saw where he was laid.'
> (Mark 15:42–47)

Jewish burial customs require the body to be buried as soon as possible on the day of death, so there was some sense of urgency. This was made worse as the Sabbath was due, and there could be no work done on the Sabbath, including burial. Pilate may have allowed the burial because he may have felt that the sooner the body was taken away the less chance there would be of any trouble.

Normally, family members and friends had to ask for the body, but it would have been very difficult for anyone to gain access to Pilate. Mark records that it was an important member of the Sanhedrin who asked Pilate for Jesus' body for burial. Joseph of Arimathea was prepared to risk the charge of sympathising with a crucified traitor from Nazareth. It is thought that he later became a Christian and may have been a source of information about Jesus' trials.

Pilate was surprised that Jesus had died already. He summoned the centurion responsible for Jesus' crucifixion to confirm that Jesus was, in fact, dead as it would often take up to three days for victims of crucifixion to die. Perhaps the beatings he had suffered earlier had sapped his energy – or was it possible that God the Father had shortened the time he suffered?

ResultsPlus
Watch out!

There are many different opinions within Christianity, so it is important never to say 'all' Christians believe something. Use adjectives such as 'most', 'many' or 'some' when describing Christian beliefs which will improve your answers.

Why was it important that Mark should record Jesus' burial?

Mark records that Joseph of Arimathea took Jesus' body and buried him, which is similar to Isaiah's prophesy: 'He was assigned a grave with the wicked, and with the rich in his death, though he had done no violence, nor was any deceit in his mouth' (Isaiah 53:9). Joseph was almost certainly rich, but the 'wicked' aspect does not seem to fit. This may suggest that Mark is historically accurate, as there is no attempt to match the story exactly with Isaiah's words.

This tomb, outside Jerusalem, is believed by some Christians to be the place where Jesus was buried.

The burial indicates that Jesus was really dead. Roman soldiers and others handling the body would not make a mistake about this. Two thousand years on, people still question whether Jesus really died on the cross. The reports of his burial encourage Christians today to believe it actually happened.

Also, by writing about it in this way Mark may have tried to avoid any arguments about where Jesus had been buried, even though there are now two sites in Jerusalem that are claimed to be the burial site. The early Christian Church had to answer charges that suggested that Jesus had not really died at all, and that the women had gone to the wrong tomb on the Sunday morning.

For discussion

What do you think about Mark's description of Jesus' burial?

Activities

1 As a highly respected member of the Sanhedrin, Joseph could be expected to 'toe the party line', but as one who was 'himself waiting for the kingdom of God', perhaps his priorities were different. What information can you find about him? Why do you think he wanted to bury Jesus?

2 **Hot-seat activity – interview with Joseph**
Choose one of the group to be interviewed as Joseph of Arimathea.

3 Explain why Jesus' burial is significant for Christians.

Summary

Joseph of Arimathea went to Pilate and asked permission to take Jesus' body down from the cross. He then took the body to a tomb and had it placed there.

3.10 The meaning and significance of the resurrection for Mark

Learning outcomes

By the end of this lesson, you should be able to:

- state the meaning of the resurrection
- give your own opinion, with a reason, about the resurrection of Jesus
- explain why the resurrection was important to Mark
- evaluate different points of view about the significance of the resurrection for Mark.

The importance of the resurrection for Mark

Jesus had been buried in the tomb since the beginning of the Sabbath (Friday night) and now it was just getting light on the Sunday morning:

'When the Sabbath was over, Mary Magdalene, Mary the mother of James, and Salome bought spices so that they might go to anoint Jesus' body. Very early on the first day of the week, just after sunrise, they were on their way to the tomb and they asked each other, "Who will roll the stone away from the entrance of the tomb?" But when they looked up, they saw that the stone, which was very large, had been rolled away. As they entered the tomb, they saw a young man dressed in a white robe sitting on the right side, and they were alarmed. "Don't be alarmed," he said. "You are looking for Jesus the Nazarene, who was crucified. He has risen! He is not here. See the place where they laid him. But go, tell his disciples and Peter, 'He is going ahead of you into Galilee. There you will see him, just as he told you.'" Trembling and bewildered, the women went out and fled from the tomb. They said nothing to anyone, because they were afraid.' (Mark 16:1–8)

Although the most reliable copies of Mark's gospel end at 16:8, many continue with another 12 verses explaining how Jesus appeared to the disciples. In ending the story with the women leaving the tomb, Mark shows the prime importance of the fact that Jesus had risen from the dead, just as he had said he would. This emphasises the importance for Mark of showing Jesus as the Messiah.

Activities

1 Look back to the table of the resurrection you began on page 61. Add more details to the table now.

Resurrection theories

Some people doubt the resurrection. They suggest theories to explain away the Christian claims. Two of the most popular are that Jesus somehow survived the crucifixion or that his disciples stole the body. However, it has been shown that surviving crucifixion and being able to walk afterwards would be a medical impossibility.

As for the theory that the disciples stole the body, there are other problems. Why would they want to steal the body in the first place? What could they hope to gain? There was no belief among the Jews that their Messiah would rise from the dead and, apart from that, in Matthew's gospel (27:64–66) there is the suggestion that an armed guard was placed outside the tomb. The disciples would have had a problem trying to carry the body away unnoticed when there were so many people in Jerusalem at the time.

If Jesus did not rise from the dead, there is still a serious question about how the body disappeared. Why would any other group want to steal the body?

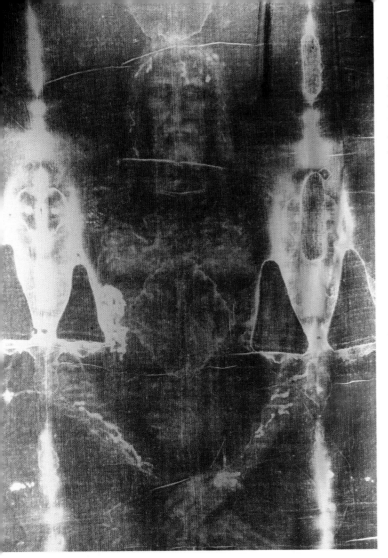

The Shroud of Turin.

left on a burial shroud. The Shroud of Turin is a long piece of linen cloth believed by millions to be the burial cloth of Jesus. This linen cloth shows a very faint image of the front and back of a human being. The shroud is preserved and kept in the cathedral in Turin, Italy, where it has been since 1578, but there are claims that its history can be traced back to its discovery, hidden in a wall in Edessa, Turkey, in 544 CE.

So why is it important?

Some scholars believe that the reason Mark finished his gospel at chapter 16 verse 8 was because he knew that his readers already understood that Jesus had risen from the dead, and any other stories of resurrection appearances might be confused with Jesus' Second Coming.

Mark wrote his gospel at a time of persecution, at a time when his readers longed for that Second Coming, as it would mean the end of their suffering. The story of the resurrection was to be an encouragement to them to persevere, as the time would come when they would 'see the Son of Man coming in clouds with great power and glory' (Mark 13:26). They could even draw comfort from the final verse, 'They said nothing to anyone, because they were afraid' (Mark 16:8), because the gospel had spread from these unpromising beginnings.

What evidence is there for the resurrection?

There is no historical evidence for the resurrection besides the claims of the disciples. No one was present to witness it, but the gospel writers all reported it. Mark has the shortest report of the resurrection, and it centres on the women finding the empty tomb. The young man in white (could he be an angel perhaps?) whom they met inside the tomb gave them the news of the resurrection.

Many churches begin their service on Easter Sunday with the chant, 'He has risen! Christ is risen indeed! Alleluia!' The Christian Church came into existence based on the disciples spreading the word of the resurrection. Many of the disciples were prepared to die for this, so it seems highly unlikely that they would have stolen the body and based the whole of Christianity on a lie.

Some Christians also believe that there is evidence of a miraculous rising from the dead in the image

Activities

2 How important do you think it is to believe in the empty tomb to understand the resurrection?

3 Does the Shroud of Turin give more grounds for belief in the resurrection?

4 Mark's gospel ends with the news that Jesus is not in the tomb but has risen. How do you think this would encourage his readers?

Summary

Women found Jesus' tomb empty and a young man in white told them that Jesus was alive. Christianity is based on the resurrection of Jesus, but there are various theories as to why the tomb was empty.

3.11 What is the meaning and significance of the resurrection for Christians today?

Learning outcomes

By the end of this lesson, you should be able to:

- state the meaning of the resurrection for Christians today
- give your own opinion, with a reason, about the meaning of the resurrection for Christians today.

Activities

1. In small groups, look back at the resurrection table on page 61. Now work out three questions about the resurrection you would ask a Christian.

2. **Hot-seat activity:**
   Using those questions, interview one member of the class (or perhaps your teacher).

The basis of Christianity

The Christian faith stands or falls with the resurrection. Paul wrote in his First Letter to the Corinthians about the many witnesses who had seen the risen Jesus. He said:

'For what I received I passed on to you as of first importance: that Christ died for our sins according to the Scriptures, that he was buried, that he was raised on the third day according to the Scriptures, and that he appeared to Peter, and then to the Twelve. After that, he appeared to more than five hundred of the brothers at the same time, most of whom are still living, though some have fallen asleep. Then he appeared to James, then to all the apostles, and last of all he appeared to me also, as to one abnormally born.' (1 Corinthians 15:3–8)

Paul then went on to explain:

'If there is no resurrection of the dead, then not even Christ has been raised. And if Christ has not been raised, our preaching is useless and so is your faith. More than that, we are then found to be false witnesses about God, for we have testified about God that he raised Christ from the dead. But he did not raise him if in fact the dead are not raised.'
(1 Corinthians 15:13–15)

Some Christians believe that the resurrection never actually happened, but that the disciples realised who Jesus was and what he had come to do only after his death. They had then been inspired to carry on his work. This view largely ignores the reports of the empty tomb and the resurrection appearances.

Another major problem with this interpretation is in the change seen in the disciples. How could they be transformed from the hopeless, frightened and disappointed men who had run away and deserted Jesus into the brave, fearless men who were prepared to die for the sake of spreading the gospel? The disciples themselves were quick to explain this change as due to Jesus being alive. This was recorded in the book of Acts several times, as for example: 'God has raised this Jesus to life, and we are all witnesses of the fact' (Acts 2:32).

Some Christians wear a crucifix like this one. This emphasises Jesus' sacrifice and suffering.

Other Christians prefer to wear an empty cross, indicating that Jesus was resurrected.

Most Christians today believe that Jesus did rise from the dead in bodily form, as they have the stories of the resurrection from all four gospels. According to these stories, the disciples touched him, talked with him and ate with him. However, there was something different about Jesus after the resurrection – he was not always recognised and he could appear in locked rooms. All Christians, then and now, would agree that Jesus is recognised, accepted and worshipped in faith, and faith is the only way to a full understanding of the risen Christ.

Easter Sunday is, to all Christians, the major day of celebration, as it focuses on the resurrection.

ResultsPlus
Watch out!

Some students get confused between Jesus' death and Jesus' resurrection – make sure you understand the difference between the two.

So, if Jesus did rise from the dead, what does that mean?

To the Christian:

- the resurrection proves the identity of Jesus as Son of God
- the resurrection confirms Jesus' work – he lived and died to bring people back to God, so they could be forgiven
- the resurrection has everyday significance too, because Jesus is alive and lives with his followers day by day
- the resurrection has brought victory over death – Jesus' triumph over death promises eternal life in the relationship enjoyed with the risen Christ now.

Activities

3 So what do you think? Is Easter the most important Christian festival that should be celebrated? Explain your answer carefully.

4 In the UK it is fairly safe to be a Christian in the 21st century, but elsewhere in the world there are Christians who face persecution daily. Do you think belief in the resurrection would help both groups of believers? Explain your answer.

For discussion

- Why is it difficult for some today to accept the resurrection?
- How do Christians answer these difficulties?

Summary

Paul says that the resurrection is the basis of Christianity. There are different attitudes to the resurrection among Christians today, but it is significant to all Christians.

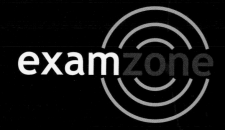

examzone

KnowZone
Death and resurrection

Quick quiz

1 What is blasphemy?

2 Where was Jesus arrested?

3 Who was Judas Iscariot?

4 Who was the chief Jewish leader at the time of Jesus?

5 Who was Pontius Pilate?

6 Where did the Last Supper take place?

7 What was the Sanhedrin?

8 Where was Jesus crucified?

9 What feast is celebrated at Passover?

10 What Jewish festival celebrates the release of the Jewish people from Egypt?

Plenary activity

Design an ideas map of all the different topics in this section on death and resurrection. The one here has been started to give you some help.

Find out more

The following books are good places to find out more:

- *Mark's gospel – An Interpretation for Today* by Robin Cooper (Hodder, ISBN 0-340-43029-X)
- *Mark: A Gospel for Today* 3rd ed by Simon and Christopher Danes (St Mark's Press, ISBN 9-781-9070-6200-1)
- *Revise GCSE Religious Studies* (Letts, ISBN-13 9-781-8431-5515-7)

You can also find out more in the Christianity section of the BBC's Religion website. Go to www.pearsonschoolsandfecolleges.co.uk/hotlinks (express code 4271P) and click on the appropriate link.

Student tips

I found it really useful to make summary tables for each topic in this section, drawing up grids to compare different points of view on each theme. In that way I was helped in answering the second question in the exam where you have to give your opinion, but it also meant that I could use the two sides of the argument in my answers to the fourth question too.

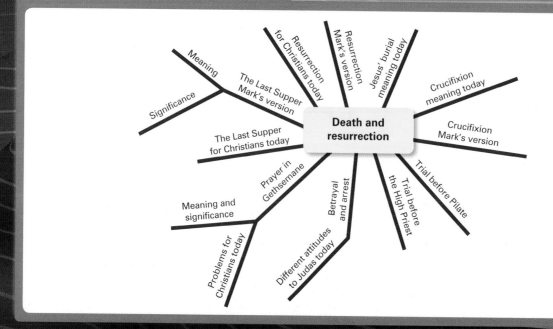

Death and resurrection

- Meaning
- Significance
- The Last Supper Mark's version
- Resurrection for Christians today
- Resurrection Mark's version
- Jesus' burial meaning today
- Crucifixion meaning today
- Crucifixion Mark's version
- The Last Supper for Christians today
- Prayer in Gethsemane
- Meaning and significance
- Problems for Christians today
- Betrayal and arrest
- Different attitudes to Judas today
- Trial before the High Priest
- Trial before Pilate

Self-evaluation checklist

How well have you understood the topics in this section? In the first column of the table below use the following code to rate your understanding:

Green – I understand this fully.

Orange – I am confident I can answer most questions on this.

Red – I need to do a lot more work on this topic.

In the second and third columns you need to think about:

- whether you have an opinion on this topic and could give reasons for that opinion if asked
- whether you can give the opinion of someone who disagrees with you and give reasons for this alternative opinion.

Content covered	My understanding is red/orange/ green	Can I give my opinion?	Can I give an alternative opinion?
The meaning and significance of the Last Supper for Mark			
Why the Last Supper is important for Christians today			
The meaning and significance of the prayers in Gethsemane			
Why they might cause problems for some Christians today			
The meaning and significance of the betrayal and arrest in Mark			
Why there are different attitudes to Judas among Christians today			
The meaning and significance of the trial before the High Priest in Mark			
How this affects Christian attitudes to justice			
The meaning and significance of the trial before Pilate in Mark			
Why Christians today may see the significance differently from Mark			
The meaning and significance of the crucifixion in Mark			
Why the crucifixion is important for Christians today			
The meaning and significance of the burial for Christians today			
The meaning and significance of the resurrection for Mark			
The meaning and significance of the resurrection for Christians today			

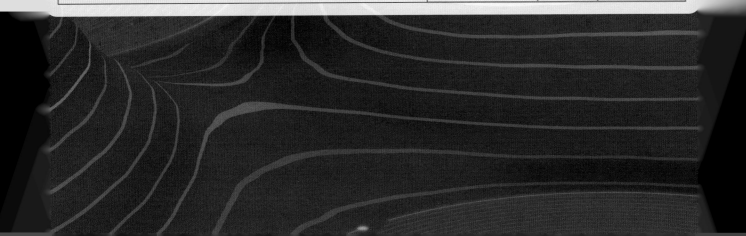

examzone

KnowZone
Death and resurrection

Introduction

In the exam you will see a choice of two questions on this section. Each question will include four tasks that test your knowledge, understanding and evaluation of the material covered. A 2-mark question will ask you to define a term; a 4-mark question will ask you to give your opinion on a point of view; an 8-mark question will ask you to explain a particular belief or idea; a 6-mark question will ask for your opinion on a point of view and ask you to consider an alternative point of view.

Here you need to give a short accurate definition. You do not need to write more than one clear sentence.

The important words in the question are 'explain why', so you must make sure that this is what you focus on in your answer. This is worth 8 marks, so you must be prepared to spend some time answering it. You will also be assessed on your use of language in this question.

As before, give reasons you have learned in class. You must show you understand why people have these other views, even if you don't agree with them.

Mini exam paper

(a) What is **Passover**? (2 marks)

(b) Do you think Jesus rose from the dead?

  Give **two** reasons for your point of view. (4 marks)

(c) Explain why the Last Supper is important for Christians today. (8 marks)

(d) 'It would have been better for Christianity if Jesus had not died.'

  In your answer you should refer to Mark's gospel and Christianity.

  (i) Do you agree? Give reasons for your opinion. (3 marks)

  (ii) Give reasons why some people may disagree with you. (3 marks)

You must give your opinion but make sure you do give two clear and properly thought-out reasons. These can be ones you have learned in class.

In your answer you should state whether you agree or disagree with the statement, and you need to support your opinion with reasons.

Mark scheme

(a) You can earn **2 marks** for a correct answer, and **1 mark** for a partially correct answer.

(b) To earn up to the full **4 marks** you need to give two reasons and develop them. Two brief reasons or only one developed reason will earn **2 marks**.

(c) You can earn **7–8 marks** by giving up to four reasons, but the fewer reasons you give, the more you must develop them. Because you are being assessed on use of language, you also need to take care to express your understanding in a clear style of English and make some use of specialist vocabulary.

(d) To go beyond **3 marks** for the whole of this question you must refer to Christianity and Mark's gospel. The more you are able to develop your reasons the more marks you will earn. Three simple reasons can earn you the same mark as one fully developed reason.

ResultsPlus
Build Better Answers

(d) 'It would have been better for Christianity if Jesus had not died.'
   In your answer you should refer to Mark's gospel and Christianity.
   (i) Do you agree? Give reasons for your opinion. (3 marks)
   (ii) Give reasons why some people may disagree with you. (3 marks)

Student answer	Comments	Improved student answer
(i) I agree with this statement, because Jesus would have lived longer and been able to teach more people his message about God. He could have founded the Church himself then, so there wouldn't be an argument about the Pope.	(i) Two simple reasons given – 2 marks. To improve this, the student needs to develop one of those reasons fully or add another simple reason.	(i) I agree with this statement, because Jesus would have lived longer and been able to teach more people his message about God. He could have founded the Church himself then, so there wouldn't be an argument about the Pope. Some people find it difficult to accept the idea that God would be shown as sacrificing his only Son.
(ii) Others disagree with this statement because they say that Mark shows that Jesus' death was predicted in his Passion words, as for example when he said, 'that the Son of Man must suffer many things and be rejected by the elders, chief priests and teachers of the law, and that he must be killed and after three days rise again'.	(ii) One developed reason – 2 marks again. To improve here would need further explanation of the reason given or another developed reason.	(ii) Others disagree with this statement because they say that Mark shows that Jesus' death was predicted in his Passion words, as for example when he said, 'that the Son of Man must suffer many things and be rejected by the elders, chief priests and teachers of the law, and that he must be killed and after three days rise again'. The crucifixion proves that Jesus was God's son as the Roman centurion said, 'Truly this man was the Son of God.'

The identity of Jesus

Introduction

In this section the key question is 'Who is Jesus?' From the start of the gospel, people who met Jesus were asking this question, and he attempted to show them who he was through his teaching and his actions. Jewish religious leaders had been searching their scriptures to find the person who would one day come from God to liberate them. Jesus based much of his teaching on those scriptures, but there was a difference between what people expected and what Jesus wanted them to see in him.

Learning outcomes for this section

By the end of this section, you should be able to:

- give definitions of the key words and use them in answers to GCSE questions
- explain what the baptism shows about Jesus for Mark and why it causes problems for some Christians today
- explain what Peter's confession at Caesarea Philippi shows about Jesus in Mark and why Matthew's record is more important for Roman Catholic Christians today
- explain what the transfiguration shows about Jesus for Mark and why it causes problems for some Christians today
- explain what the calming of the storm shows about Jesus for Mark and why it causes problems for some Christians today
- explain what the feeding of the five thousand shows about Jesus for Mark and why it causes problems for some Christians today
- explain what the walking on the sea shows about Jesus for Mark and why it causes problems for some Christians today
- explain what the healing of Legion shows about Jesus for Mark and why it causes problems for some Christians today
- explain what the raising of Jairus' daughter shows about Jesus for Mark and why it causes problems for some Christians today
- explain what the title 'Messiah' shows about Jesus and its significance for Christians today
- explain what the title 'Son of Man' shows about Jesus and its significance for Christians today
- explain why reading Mark's gospel leads some people to believe that Jesus was the Son of God.

edexcel ⠿ key terms

baptism	healing miracle	Legion	nature miracle
confession	Jairus	Messiah	Son of Man
Elijah	John the Baptist	Moses	transfiguration

1 In groups of two or three, look at the images of Jesus shown here.
- In what ways are they alike in their portrayal of Jesus?
- In what ways are they different?
- Which do you think might be the closest likeness to Jesus?

2 Is it easier for Christians to understand the gospel if they have a mental picture of what Jesus looked like, even if it is the wrong picture?

4.1 Jesus is baptised

Learning outcomes

By the end of this lesson, you should be able to:

- state the meaning of the word 'baptism'
- give your own opinion, with a reason, as to why Jesus was baptised
- explain what the baptism shows about Jesus for Mark and why baptism was important for Mark in writing his gospel
- express your own point of view, giving your reasons, for why the baptism of Jesus causes problems for some Christians today
- evaluate different points of view about the practice of baptism for Christians today.

John the Baptist

The Old Testament prophet Isaiah, writing some 400 years before Jesus' birth, predicts the arrival of a messenger who will prepare the ground for the Messiah's arrival. In Mark's gospel, **John the Baptist** appears in the desert. He wears outlandish clothes and eats a strange diet, but many people come to hear him speak.

'It is written in Isaiah the prophet: "I will send my messenger ahead of you, who will prepare your way" – "a voice of one calling in the desert, 'Prepare the way for the Lord, make straight paths for him.'" And so John came, baptizing in the desert region and preaching a baptism of repentance for the forgiveness of sins. The whole Judean countryside and all the people of Jerusalem went out to him. Confessing their sins, they were baptized by him in the Jordan River. John wore clothing made of camel's hair, with a leather belt around his waist, and he ate locusts and wild honey. And this was his message: "After me will come one more powerful than I, the thongs of whose sandals I am not worthy to stoop down and untie. I baptize you with water, but he will baptize you with the Holy Spirit."'
(Mark 1:2–8)

edexcel ⦂⦂⦂ key terms

baptism – Confessing sins and being immersed in water as a sign of purification.

John the Baptist – The man who baptised Jesus in the river Jordan.

John's preaching and the **baptism** he offered were intended to call the people to prepare themselves for the coming of the Messiah. His baptism would have involved dipping a person under the water in the River Jordan. It would have been a familiar act for the Jews, as they regularly took ritual baths to make them 'clean' and 'pure' of the things that separated them from God. The Jewish Law required this ritual bathing to be in running water. Entry into the water would symbolise putting things right. For John, baptism is about people repenting of their sins and God forgiving them. Dipping them in water symbolises that their sins have been 'washed away'. The idea of being immersed in water is carried forward by John to symbolise Jesus immersing a person in the Holy Spirit.

Jesus' baptism

'At that time Jesus came from Nazareth in Galilee and was baptized by John in the Jordan. As Jesus was coming up out of the water, he saw heaven being torn open and the Spirit descending on him like a dove. And a voice came from heaven: "You are my Son, whom I love; with you I am well pleased."'
(Mark 1:9–11)

Mark saw this baptism as the starting point of Jesus' ministry. He portrays it as a supernatural event that shows that Jesus is special. The Holy Spirit descends on Jesus and God the Father speaks to him. It is the first time that Jesus appears in the gospel, and Mark wants to show that God the Father calls Jesus his son, whom he loves. Christians believe that God is three persons, called the Trinity, but only one God (see page 115). The Holy Spirit is the third person of the Trinity –

so here all three members are shown together, with the God the Father giving his approval to Jesus, his son. Mark also uses this baptism to show the importance of John's teaching.

Activities

1   Do you think it is important to have an initiation ceremony? Give reasons for your answer.

2   Explain in your own words why Jesus' baptism is important to Mark.

Christian baptism today

As a Jew, Jesus would have practised this form of ritual cleansing. At the time of Pentecost, Jesus' disciples baptised people after they had received the Holy Spirit (Acts 2). Today, most Christians use baptism. They do this to follow the example of Jesus and the disciples, and to show they want to become Christians. Some believe that at baptism, as someone becomes a Christian, the Holy Spirit enters the person to give them new life.

Baptism is usually seen as a sacrament – the outward physical sign of an inward invisible grace. Christians believe that, since the time that Adam and Eve ate the forbidden fruit in the Garden of Eden (Genesis 3), all humanity has been born in a state of Original Sin. When someone is baptised by immersion in water or sprinkling with water and a priest or minister says the blessing 'in the name of the Father, the Son and the Holy Spirit', this Original Sin is washed away.

Activities

3   Research task: go to www.heinemann. co.uk/hotlinks (express code 4271P) and the appropriate links to find out about different churches' approaches to: a) infant baptism and b) believers' baptism.

4   Discuss in small groups of three or four the advantages and disadvantages of these two approaches to baptism.

5   Write a summary of your discussion, showing that you have thought about both approaches, but come to a conclusion about which you would prefer.

Christians baptise in different ways and may disagree about when in a person's life baptism should take place.

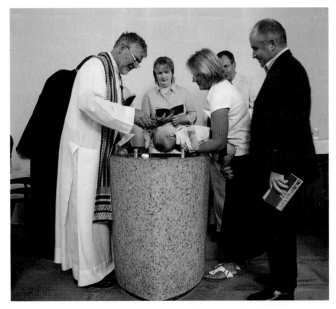

Many Christians, such as Roman Catholics and Anglicans, practise infant baptism, where babies are baptised inside a church. Godparents are invited to make promises on behalf of the baby, which can then be confirmed when the child grows up.

Some Protestant Churches, such as the Baptists, practise believers' baptism, where adults are baptised by being immersed in water, usually inside a church. Some Christians still baptise adults in running water, in a similar way to how Jesus was baptised by John the Baptist.

Summary

The baptism of Jesus by John the Baptist is shown by Mark as the beginning of Jesus' ministry. Different Christian denominations have different beliefs about the practice of baptism and this can cause problems for some Christians today.

4.2 Peter at Caesarea Philippi

Learning outcomes

By the end of this lesson, you should be able to:

- state the meaning of confession
- give your own opinion, with a reason, about what Peter's confession shows about Jesus
- explain why Matthew's gospel record of Peter's confession is more important for Catholic Christians today and express your own point of view on this
- evaluate different points of view about Peter's role in the Church.

edexcel ⠿ key terms

confession – An acknowledgement or declaration of something.

Elijah – The Old Testament prophet believed to return before the Messiah.

Messiah – The Anointed One (Christ) who would bring in God's Kingdom.

Activities

1 Look at this poster – unfortunately, the job description is not available, so in pairs, decide what qualifications and experience you would look for in a **Messiah**.

Work For Us!

WE'RE LOOKING FOR THE MESSIAH, ALIAS
THE CHRIST

FULL JOB DESCRIPTION AVAILABLE ON APPLICATION

Peter's confession

'Jesus and his disciples went on to the villages around Caesarea Philippi. On the way he asked them, "Who do people say I am?" They replied, "Some say John the Baptist; others say **Elijah**; and still others, one of the prophets." "But what about you?" he asked. "Who do you say I am?" Peter answered, "You are the Christ."

'Jesus warned them not to tell anyone about him. He then began to teach them that the Son of Man must suffer many things and be rejected by the elders, chief priests and teachers of the law, and that he must be killed and after three days rise again. He spoke plainly about this, and Peter took him aside and began to rebuke him. But when Jesus turned and looked at his disciples, he rebuked Peter. "Get behind me, Satan!" he said. "You do not have in mind the things of God, but the things of men."'
(Mark 8:27–33)

For discussion

From this passage, discuss these questions:

- What do some people think about who Jesus is?
- Who does Peter believe Jesus is?
- Why do you think Jesus warns the disciples not to tell anyone?
- Jesus' response to Peter seems harsh. Why do you think he tells Peter to 'Get behind me, Satan!'

'When Jesus came to the region of Caesarea Philippi, he asked his disciples, "Who do people say the Son of Man is?" They replied, "Some say John the Baptist; others say Elijah; and still others, Jeremiah or one of the prophets." "But what about you?" he asked. "Who do you say I am?" Simon Peter answered, "You are the Christ, the Son of the living God." Jesus replied, "Blessed are you, Simon son of Jonah, for this was not revealed to you by man, but by my Father in heaven. And I tell you that you are Peter, and on this rock I will build my church, and the gates of Hades will not overcome it. I will give you the keys of the kingdom of heaven; whatever you bind on earth will be bound in heaven, and whatever you loose on earth will be loosed in heaven." Then he warned his disciples not to tell anyone that he was the Christ.' (Matthew 16:13–20)

This passage is important because it gives readers information on how Jesus' teachings were being received at the time. John the Baptist had a reputation for his teaching, while Elijah was a very important prophet in Judaism (see pages 98–99). More importantly, Peter's **confession** is the first time that someone recognises Jesus as the Christ, the Messiah (see pages 110–111). However, in this account Peter does not seem to understand the meaning of 'Messiah' in the same way as Jesus. The Jewish Messiah was traditionally seen as someone who would be a warrior-king. Therefore, Peter did not like Jesus' predictions of a suffering Messiah, but Jesus felt strongly that this was his mission.

Matthew's version of the story

The Roman Catholic Church teaches that this event marked the appointment of Peter as the first Pope – the person who would lead the Christian Church after Jesus' ascension into heaven. This same story told in Matthew's gospel shows why they make this claim:

Roman Catholics point to the name Peter, as *petros* is also the Greek word for 'rock', so that when Jesus said that 'On this rock I will build my church', he meant that the Church would be built from Peter's leadership. He thus became the first Pope. Other Christian denominations believe that Peter was the leader of the disciples when Jesus left, but he shared the responsibility for the Church with others like Paul. To them, the rock would be Jesus himself.

The current Pope, Benedict XVI, claims to be the latest successor to St Peter in the line of Popes who have led the Roman Catholic Church for the past 2,000 years. Reading the two versions of the story shows the grounds for this view.

Activities

2 Why do you think Peter is identified as the leader of the Church?
3 Explain why, for Roman Catholics, Matthew's record of this event is more important than Mark's.

Summary

Peter recognised that Jesus was the Christ, the Messiah, when Jesus asked who people thought he was. Roman Catholics feel that the account of the story in Matthew's gospel is more important because they believe that Peter was their first Pope.

4.3 The transfiguration

98

Learning outcomes

By the end of this lesson, you should be able to:

- state the meaning of the word 'transfiguration'
- give your own opinion, with a reason, about what the transfiguration shows about Jesus
- explain why the transfiguration may cause problems for some Christians today

Activities

1 Read Exodus 34:29–35. What does this passage tell you about what happened to **Moses** when he came down from the mountain after he had been talking to God? Now read 2 Kings 2:11 and see what happened to Elijah. Remember these events as you read this next passage from Mark. Afterwards, discuss what connection you can see between these incidents.

The transfiguration

edexcel ⠿ **key terms**

Moses – The Old Testament prophet to whom God gave his laws.

transfiguration – When Jesus' appearance was changed.

'And he said to them, "I tell you the truth, some who are standing here will not taste death before they see the kingdom of God come with power."

'After six days Jesus took Peter, James and John with him and led them up a high mountain, where they were all alone. There he was transfigured before them. His clothes became dazzling white, whiter than anyone in the world could bleach them. And there appeared before them Elijah and Moses, who were talking with Jesus. Peter said to Jesus, "Rabbi, it is good for us to be here. Let us put up three shelters – one for you, one for Moses and one for Elijah." He did not know what to say, they were so frightened. Then a cloud appeared and enveloped them, and a voice came from the cloud: "This is my Son, whom I love. Listen to him!" Suddenly, when they looked around, they no longer saw anyone with them except Jesus. As they were coming down the mountain, Jesus gave them orders not to tell anyone what they had seen until the Son of Man had risen from the dead. They kept the matter to themselves, discussing what "rising from the dead" meant.'
(Mark 9:1–10)

The Transfiguration of Christ on Mount Tabor *(1478) by Giovanni Bellini. The two people standing with Jesus are Moses and Elijah, while the three disciples can be seen crouched in the foreground.*

Mark has included this story because he sees it as an important pointer to the question 'Who is Jesus?' It takes place six days after Peter's confession that Jesus is 'the Christ'.

Jesus goes through a **transfiguration**, which means there was a supernatural change in the way he looked. Mark describes Jesus' clothes dazzling white, with Jesus shining in a way they had not experienced before. To Mark this was something wonderful and awesome, with Jesus displaying an authority that was more than human – nothing less than an experience of the glory of God.

The other characters who appear with Jesus are important Old Testament prophets. Moses received the Ten Commandments from God and Elijah challenged 450 prophets of Baal – and won. Their appearance shows Jesus as continuing or fulfilling the line of the Old Testament prophets and therefore of Judaism.

As Mark reports it, there is also a parallel between Jesus' baptism (see pages 94–95) and the transfiguration. In both cases, God the Father speaks to emphasise who Jesus is. In this case God says, 'This is my Son, whom I love. Listen to him!'

Problems for Christians today?

Some Christians find this story difficult to accept at face value. They wonder how characters from hundreds of years before could actually appear with Jesus. They suggest that the disciples may have had a vision of the event. Others take it literally, for 'nothing is impossible with God' (Luke 1:37). Elijah was an important figure in the Jewish understanding of the Messiah, as the prophet Malachi had foretold that he would return before the coming of the Messiah to prepare the way for him.

Peter's response in offering to put up three tents suggests that he did not really understand what was happening and did not know what to say.

Build Better Answers

'The disciples must have imagined they heard God talking to them.'
In your answer you should refer to Mark's gospel and Roman Catholic Christianity.
(i) Do you agree? Give reasons for your opinion. (3 marks)
(ii) Give reasons why some people may disagree with you. (3 marks)
Comments refer to both parts.

■ **Basic, 1-mark answers**
These answers will offer an opinion with a simple reason.

● **Good, 2-mark answers**
Good answers will either give two simple reasons for their opinion or one developed reason.

▲ **Excellent, 3-mark answers**
The best answers will either give three simple reasons, two developed reasons, or one fully developed reason for their opinion.

Activities

2 **Hot-seat activity – interview with Peter.**
You, Peter, have just returned from the transfiguration. The other disciples are eager to know what has happened. Imagine your feelings and how you can describe them to the others. (If you find this difficult, perhaps include James and John in the hot-seat to share the questions.)

For discussion

- Do you think it matters whether the transfiguration of Jesus was an actual event or a vision that took place in the minds of the disciples?
- Why do you think Jesus tells them to keep quiet about it?

Summary

Jesus was transfigured in front of his three closest disciples. Elijah and Moses appeared alongside Jesus and God announced that Jesus is 'my Son, whom I love. Listen to him!' The disciples were puzzled about what it all meant.

4.4 Jesus calms a storm

Learning outcomes

By the end of this lesson, you should be able to:

● describe the story of the storm

● give your own opinion, with a reason, about what the calming of the storm shows about Jesus for Mark

● explain why the story may cause problems for some Christians today and express your own point of view

● evaluate different points of view about the meaning of the story of the storm.

Activities

1 Some people think that this description of the calming of a storm includes one or two details that could have come only from an eyewitness, and that would be the disciple Peter. As you read the story, see if you can find those details.

'That day when evening came, he said to his disciples, "Let us go over to the other side." Leaving the crowd behind, they took him along, just as he was, in the boat. There were also other boats with him. A furious squall came up, and the waves broke over the boat, so that it was nearly swamped. Jesus was in the stern, sleeping on a cushion. The disciples woke him and said to him, "Teacher, don't you care if we drown?" He got up, rebuked the wind and said to the waves, "Quiet! Be still!" Then the wind died down and it was completely calm. He said to his disciples, "Why are you so afraid? Do you still have no faith?" They were terrified and asked each other, "Who is this? Even the wind and the waves obey him!"'
(Mark 4:35–41)

edexcel ⠿ key terms

nature miracle – A miracle in which Jesus shows his power over nature.

This is Mark's first account of a **nature miracle.** These squalls (storms) are a feature of the Sea of Galilee, so the fishermen would not have been surprised by a storm, although this one was particularly strong. Not all the disciples had been fisherman either.

With just a few words from Jesus the storm stopped – the wind died down and the waves became a flat calm. This was scary for the disciples, but Jesus was surprised at them. 'Do you still have no faith?' he asked. Mark uses this story to show the power of Jesus. It only takes a few words from Jesus for the raging storm to stop and the waves to settle to a flat calm.

Jesus Calms the Storm *(1633) by Rembrandt.*

Activities

2 Jesus was asleep in the boat. What does this suggest about Jesus' attitude to the storm?

3 After they had seen what Jesus did, what question did the disciples ask?

4 Pretend that you are one of the disciples in the boat with Jesus. Write a diary extract explaining what happened. What did you learn about Jesus from this event?

Why does this create problems for some Christians today?

While most Christians believe that God has the power to do anything, some find it very difficult to believe this particular story. Nature miracles are, for many people, the most difficult to accept, as they seem to go against the laws of nature. How can storms be stilled? Some believe that modern scientific knowledge casts doubt on whether the story really happened.

These people may interpret the miracle as an allegory, where the storm represents the persecution faced by Christians at the time Mark was writing.

In Old Testament times the sea had been a symbol for chaos that could be overcome only by God, as in this psalm:

> 'Then they cried out to the Lord in their trouble, and he brought them out of their distress. He stilled the storm to a whisper; the waves of the sea were hushed. They were glad when it grew calm, and he guided them to their desired haven.'
> (Psalm 107:28–30)

Perhaps Mark is using the same device in his telling of the calming of the storm. Those who cry out for help can be assured that Jesus is in control and will steer the persecuted Christian boat into calmer seas.

Christians in the UK today have little to fear from persecution, although this is not true for many across the world. The 'storms' of persecution continue for them. All Christians believe that Jesus helps and guides them through the 'storms of life', so whether Jesus really was able to calm a storm may not be important for them.

Activities

5 Early Christians sometimes suffered persecution. Explain what encouragement they could receive from this event.

 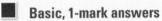

ResultsPlus
Build Better Answers

Do you think that Jesus really calmed a storm?

Give **two** reasons for your point of view. (4 marks)

▪ **Basic, 1-mark answers**
Answers will give their opinion but with just one basic reason.

● **Good, 2–3-mark answers**
Answers that receive 2 marks will give their opinion with either two basic or one developed reason.

▲ **Excellent, 4-mark answers**
The best answers will give their opinion supported by two developed reasons.

Summary

Jesus and the disciples were sailing across the Sea of Galilee when a sudden fierce storm blew up. Jesus calmed the storm with a few words. The Church interprets this story in terms of the storms of life – and how Jesus guides people through them to safety.

4.5 The feeding of the five thousand

Learning outcomes

By the end of this lesson, you should be able to:

● describe the story of the feeding of the five thousand

● give your own opinion, with a reason, about what the feeding shows about Jesus

● explain why the story may cause problems for some Christians today and express your own point of view

● evaluate different points of view about the meaning of the story of the feeding.

Activities

1 Look up the following stories where God miraculously provides food for people in the Old Testament and make a summary of them:

● Exodus 16

● 2 Kings 4:42–44.

The feeding of the five thousand

'So they went away by themselves in a boat to a solitary place. But many who saw them leaving recognised them and ran on foot from all the towns and got there ahead of them. When Jesus landed and saw a large crowd, he had compassion on them, because they were like sheep without a shepherd. So he began teaching them many things. By this time it was late in the day, so his disciples came to him. "This is a remote place," they said, "and it's already very late. Send the people away so they can go to the surrounding countryside and villages and buy themselves something to eat." But he answered, "You give them something to eat."

'They said to him, "That would take eight months of a man's wages! Are we to go and spend that much on bread and give it to them to eat?" "How many loaves do you have?" he asked. "Go and see." When they found out, they said, "Five – and two fish." Then Jesus directed them to have all the people sit down in groups on the green grass. So they sat down in groups of hundreds and fifties. Taking the five loaves and the two fish and looking up to heaven, he gave thanks and broke the loaves. Then he gave them to his disciples to set before the people. He also divided the two fish among them all. They all ate and were satisfied, and the disciples picked up twelve basketfuls of broken pieces of bread and fish. The number of the men who had eaten was five thousand.' (Mark 6:32–44)

This is another example of a nature miracle, for here food is miraculously multiplied from five loaves and two fish to enough for 5,000 men (and some say there would have been women and children as well). Mark has included this story to show the power of Jesus. When he reported this miracle, Mark would have been aware of the Old Testament stories of God feeding the Israelites in the desert, so some people believe that he wanted to show Jesus' power to feed people miraculously too. He is directly linking Jesus' power with God's power.

Christians today

There are different views about what actually happened – here are some of them:

People in the crowd saw that Jesus was willing to share his food with them, so they felt guilty and shared their food too.

People only really got a small scrap of bread each.

Could anyone else have conjured up enough food for this number?

Maybe it was all made up to illustrate a 'message'.

Perhaps Mark exaggerated the numbers – what if there were only a few people?

What if Jesus really did feed 5,000 men with just five loaves and two fish?

Activities

2 If it did happen in the way Mark has reported, what does that suggest about Jesus?

3 What do you think happened? Do you agree with any of these thought bubbles?

Some Christians may find it difficult to accept that this miracle could have happened because it is so incredible for 5,000 people to be fed on such little food. They might think that the story is an exaggeration to show Jesus' power. However, others may say that it does not really matter whether the story is historically accurate, the most important thing that can be learned from it is to care for others and to share. They may see it as teaching that Christians should always try to help others and not be greedy.

Activities

4 'The problem for some Christians is that there are still millions who are starving across the world today – why aren't they fed?' How would you answer this criticism?

Challenge

5 At the end of his life, Jesus and his disciples ate a Last Supper together. At the meal he broke bread, handed it round, and said that it was his body. He gave them wine too and said that this was his blood.

- In what ways could the feeding of the 5,000 be thought to foreshadow the Last Supper?

- Do you think there is any significance in the twelve baskets of scraps collected afterwards?

Summary

Jesus fed a large crowd of 5,000 men in a nature miracle, using five loaves and two small fish. The left-overs filled twelve baskets.

4.6 Jesus walks on the sea

Learning outcomes

By the end of this lesson, you should be able to:

- describe the story of Jesus walking on the sea according to Mark
- give your own opinion, with a reason, about what this incident shows about Jesus
- evaluate different points of view about the miracle
- explain why the story may cause problems for some Christians today and express your own point of view.

Activities

In the last two topics we have been looking at miracles performed by Jesus, and we will have some more stories shortly. Discuss with your partner these questions:

1 What do you think makes a miracle?

2 Do miracles happen nowadays?

3 Why do you think Jesus performed miracles?

Peter Walks on Water *(1806) by Philipp Otto Runge.*

Another nature miracle

Mark links the story of the feeding of the 5,000 to this next story, another demonstration of nature being tamed. In this way he knows that people will be sure to make the connection that Jesus had that power.

'Immediately Jesus made his disciples get into the boat and go on ahead of him to Bethsaida, while he dismissed the crowd. After leaving them, he went up on a mountainside to pray. When evening came, the boat was in the middle of the lake, and he was alone on land. He saw the disciples straining at the oars, because the wind was against them. About the fourth watch of the night he went out to them, walking on the lake. He was about to pass by them, but when they saw him walking on the lake, they thought he was a ghost. They cried out, because they all saw him and were terrified.

'Immediately he spoke to them and said, "Take courage! It is I. Don't be afraid." Then he climbed into the boat with them, and the wind died down. They were completely amazed, for they had not understood about the loaves; their hearts were hardened.'
(Mark 6:45–52)

This story is similar in some ways to the calming of the storm. Both take place on the Sea of Galilee, with the disciples in a boat. Jesus' ministry at the time was based in the towns and villages around the lake and four of his disciples had been fishermen, so it would not be unusual for them to use a boat.

Then Jesus surprised them by walking to them across the water. The last verse says that they were completely amazed, 'for they had not understood about the loaves'. The loaves had been a demonstration of Jesus' power over nature, and this nature miracle is further evidence of this. The image of God walking over the sea appears in Psalm 77:19: 'Your path led through the sea, your way through the mighty waters, though your footprints were not seen.' Jesus says to the disciples, 'Take courage! It is I. Don't be afraid.' The Greek words for 'It is I' are simply 'I am', and this is what God calls himself in Exodus 3:14 when he speaks to Moses at the burning bush. So again, Mark is linking Jesus to God and showing his power.

Activities

4 Write a summary of the nature miracles performed by Jesus in Mark's gospel. What are the similarities and differences between the stories? What do they each show about Jesus for Mark?

Why this story may cause problems for some Christians today

Christians might find problems with this story because everyone knows human beings cannot walk on water. They might find it difficult to understand why Jesus did this. The disciples were experienced fishermen so they were probably not at any real risk from the wind. However, Christians may believe that the story is teaching people that they should believe in Jesus' powers and not be like the disciples who 'had not understood about the loaves' and whose 'hearts were hardened'.

What alternative explanations are there? Here are some ideas that have been put forward:

- Jesus was walking near the sea, and not on it. The Greek word used could mean 'close by' as well as 'on'.

- The disciples made a mistake. Jesus was not really walking on the water. There was a hidden reef or a raft perhaps.
- Maybe Mark made it up to illustrate a link between Jesus and the Old Testament.
- Many Christians believe that it happened just as Mark reported.

ResultsPlus
Build Better Answers

'Jesus can't have performed nature miracles – Mark must have made them up.'

In your answer you should refer to Mark's gospel and Christianity.

(i) Do you agree? Give reasons for your answer (3 marks)

(ii) Give reasons why some people may disagree with you. (3 marks)

Note: these comments refer to both parts.

 Basic, 1-mark answers
These answers offer a simple comment.

 Good, 2-mark answers
These will either give two simple reasons or one developed reason.

▲ **Excellent, 3-mark answers**
The best answers will give either three simple reasons, two developed reasons or one fully developed reason.

Summary

Jesus walked across the sea to join his disciples as they were travelling in a boat. They were fearful, thinking it was a ghost they had seen. Mark linked the incident, along with Jesus' words of reassurance, to Old Testament pictures of God appearing to his people.

4.7 Jesus heals Legion

Learning outcomes

By the end of this lesson, you should be able to:

- describe the story of Jesus healing Legion by casting out the demons as Mark reports it
- give your own opinion, with a reason, about what this incident shows about Jesus
- evaluate different points of view about the miracle and come to your own conclusions
- explain why the story may cause problems for some Christians today.

edexcel ⠿ key terms

Legion – A man from whom Jesus cast out many demons.

Activities

1 Go through this story again, one section at a time. Note down anything the account is saying or implying about Jesus as you read.

Jesus heals Legion

We are now going to look at an example of Jesus healing a man by exorcising demons:

'They went across the lake to the region of the Gerasenes. When Jesus got out of the boat, a man with an evil spirit came from the tombs to meet him. This man lived in the tombs, and no one could bind him any more, not even with a chain. For he had often been chained hand and foot, but he tore the chains apart and broke the irons on his feet. No one was strong enough to subdue him. Night and day among the tombs and in the hills he would cry out and cut himself with stones.

'When he saw Jesus from a distance, he ran and fell on his knees in front of him. He shouted at the top of his voice, "What do you want with me, Jesus, Son of the Most High God? Swear to God that you won't torture me!" For Jesus had said to him, "Come out of this man, you evil spirit!"

'Then Jesus asked him, "What is your name?" "My name is **Legion**," he replied, "for we are many." And he begged Jesus again and again not to send them out of the area. A large herd of pigs was feeding on the nearby hillside. The demons begged Jesus, "Send us among the pigs; allow us to go into them." He gave them permission, and the evil spirits came out and went into the pigs. The herd, about two thousand in number, rushed down the steep bank into the lake and were drowned.

'Those tending the pigs ran off and reported this in the town and countryside, and the people went out to see what had happened. When they came to Jesus, they saw the man who had been possessed by the legion of demons, sitting there, dressed and in his right mind; and they were afraid. Those who had seen it told the people what had happened to the demon-possessed man – and told about the pigs as well. Then the people began to plead with Jesus to leave their region.

'As Jesus was getting into the boat, the man who had been demon-possessed begged to go with him. Jesus did not let him, but said, "Go home to your family and tell them how much the Lord has done for you, and how he has had mercy on you." So the man went away and began to tell in the Decapolis how much Jesus had done for him. And all the people were amazed.'
(Mark 5:1–20)

What does this show about Jesus?

- The man believed he was possessed by evil spirits and Jesus removed them – this shows that Jesus has power over evil.
- The man (or is it the demons that possess him?) recognises who Jesus is – 'Son of the Most High God'.
- Jesus would free a human life from the power of Satan at any cost – in this case at the cost of a whole herd of pigs.
- Whatever was wrong with Legion, Jesus had the power to heal him.
- The people are amazed by this tale, but they are also afraid of Jesus' power.

Perhaps the story of the pigs was added later as a veiled criticism of the Romans, who the Jews thought were no better than pigs.

Jesus made the pigs stampede to convince the man that he had been cured. He had believed he was possessed by demons and needed to see proof.

Jesus didn't mean to kill the pigs, but they were frightened into stampeding by the violent fit the man had as Jesus healed him.

It was the demons that killed the pigs, not Jesus.

What about the poor farmer? Jesus doesn't show much respect for him.

Human life is more valuable than an animal – especially an unclean animal like a pig.

For discussion

- Why do you think people at the time of Jesus thought that mental illness was caused by demonic possession?
- Do people still believe in possession by evil spirits today?

Activities

2 What do you think? Do you agree with any of these thought bubbles?

Explain your own idea of what happened.

Why this causes problems for some Christians

Mental illness still poses problems for some people today. Somehow it seems worse than physical illness, although there are rational explanations for many mental conditions, just as there are for physical ones. The idea of possession by evil spirits is one that many discount as superstition, and that includes many Christians. Others still remain convinced of the reality of demons and spirits.

The other aspect of this incident that may cause problems for some is the way Jesus treats the pigs. Here are some ideas about this:

Summary

Jesus healed Legion, who was possessed by evil spirits, sending them into a herd of pigs nearby. This may cause problems for Christians because they may not believe in demonic possession or it may cause problems because of the way Jesus treats the pigs.

4.8 The raising of Jairus' daughter

Learning outcomes

By the end of this lesson, you should be able to:

- describe the story of Jesus raising Jairus' daughter from death
- give your own opinion, with a reason, about what the healing of Jairus' daughter shows about Jesus
- evaluate different points of view about this miracle and express your own opinions with reasons
- explain why this story may cause problems for some Christians today.

edexcel ⠿ key terms

healing miracle – A miracle in which Jesus shows his power over sickness.

Jairus – The synagogue ruler whose daughter was brought back to life by Jesus.

Jesus shows power over death

'When Jesus had again crossed over by boat to the other side of the lake, a large crowd gathered around him while he was by the lake. Then one of the synagogue rulers, named **Jairus**, came there. Seeing Jesus, he fell at his feet and pleaded earnestly with him, "My little daughter is dying. Please come and put your hands on her so that she will be healed and live." So Jesus went with him.

'A large crowd followed and pressed around him. And a woman was there who had been subject to bleeding for twelve years. She had suffered a great deal under the care of many doctors and had spent all she had, yet instead of getting better she grew worse. When she heard about Jesus, she came up behind him in the crowd and touched his cloak, because she thought, "If I just touch his clothes, I will be healed." Immediately her bleeding stopped and she felt in her body that she was freed from her suffering. At once Jesus realized that power had gone out from him. He turned around in the crowd and asked, "Who touched my clothes?"

'"You see the people crowding against you," his disciples answered, "and yet you can ask, 'Who touched me?'"

'But Jesus kept looking around to see who had done it. Then the woman, knowing what had happened to her,

came and fell at his feet and, trembling with fear, told him the whole truth. He said to her, "Daughter, your faith has healed you. Go in peace and be freed from your suffering."

'While Jesus was still speaking, some men came from the house of Jairus, the synagogue ruler. "Your daughter is dead," they said. "Why bother the teacher any more?" Ignoring what they said, Jesus told the synagogue ruler, "Don't be afraid; just believe."

'He did not let anyone follow him except Peter, James and John the brother of James. When they came to the home of the synagogue ruler, Jesus saw a commotion, with people crying and wailing loudly. He went in and said to them, "Why all this commotion and wailing? The child is not dead but asleep." But they laughed at him. After he put them all out, he took the child's father and mother and the disciples who were with him, and went in where the child was. He took her by the hand and said to her, "Talitha koum!" (which means, "Little girl, I say to you, get up!"). Immediately the girl stood up and walked around (she was twelve years old). At this they were completely astonished. He gave strict orders not to let anyone know about this, and told them to give her something to eat.'
(Mark 5:21–43)

The Resurrection of Jairus' Daughter *(1871) by Ilja Repin.*

By now many Jewish leaders were openly critical of Jesus, so the leader of the local synagogue (Jairus) would have had to be desperate to be seen asking Jesus for help. His daughter was obviously very ill. On the way to Jairus' house Jesus performed a **healing miracle** on a woman with a haemorrhage, and it then seemed as though it was too late to save Jairus' daughter, as she was dead.

The fact that there were lots of people in the house could be taken by readers as proof that the girl was really dead – they can't all be wrong. Similarly, Jesus telling her parents to give her something to eat would suggest that she was really cured.

This story shows Jesus' ability to heal people. Early Christians valued such stories as this, for they offered proof that they were following their Messiah. This miracle in particular shows not just Jesus' ability to heal people but that he actually had power over life and death. Eventually, of course, Jesus himself came back from the dead.

Problems for today

Christians today are divided in their understanding of the story of Jairus' daughter. Many people may believe it happened exactly as reported, with Jesus raising the girl from the dead. Others might think that when Jesus said she was only sleeping that this is exactly what he meant. However, it seems unlikely that Mark would report the incident if it was just this. Jesus' action in raising her was *like* waking someone who was asleep, and Mark would have understood Jesus saying she was asleep rather than dead. Some people may question why Jesus chose to bring this girl back from the dead rather than others.

Other Christians might feel that it is not necessary to believe that the story is true. They would say that the story was told to illustrate the point that Jesus was special and to point towards Jesus' own resurrection.

For discussion

Was Jairus' daughter really dead? What did Jesus mean when he said she was only asleep? Does it make any difference to the way we see the miracle performed?

Activities

1 Complete the news report under this title:

GALILEE GUARDIAN

Miracle worker heals two

'Jesus – the well-known rabbi from Nazareth – is reported to have been involved in amazing events today...'

Summary

Jesus raised Jairus' daughter from death. This was the first indication that Jesus had power over death, and it pointed to his own resurrection.

4.9 Jesus – the Messiah

Learning outcomes

By the end of this lesson, you should be able to:

- describe the use of the title 'Messiah' for Jesus
- give your own opinion, with a reason, about what this title shows about Jesus
- explain the significance of the title for Christians today

Activities

1 Look back to the stories of the transfiguration and Peter's confession (pages 98–99):

- Who were the Old Testament people who were with Jesus?
- How did the presence of these people suggest that Jesus was the Messiah?
- What did Peter say he believed about Jesus?
- Why did some people think that Jesus might be Elijah or John the Baptist come back from the dead?

Mosaic of Jesus Christ in the Church of Sant'Apollinare Nuovo, Ravenna, Italy.

Meaning of 'Messiah'

The names 'Messiah', 'Christ' and 'Anointed One' all mean the same, the difference being that 'Messiah' is the Hebrew word for 'anointed one' and 'Christ' is the Greek word. As such: 'Christ' is a title given to Jesus, and not his surname. The gospel of Mark opens with this: 'The beginning of the gospel about Jesus Christ, the Son of God' (Mark 1:1), showing that from the start Mark is anxious to identify Jesus as the Messiah.

In Israel, the high priests and kings had been anointed with oil to indicate that they had been chosen and appointed by God to these positions. The picture of a Messiah figure developed slowly – he was someone who would come in the future to restore Israel's fortunes, a descendant of David, chosen by God to rule as King. He would bring peace and establish God's rule over the Earth.

At this point there was no clear idea of how God would bring the Messiah into the world, but there were four main beliefs:

- the Messiah, God's representative, was to stand against God's enemies and the enemies of his chosen people
- all faithful Jews would be brought back to their homeland from exile
- Jerusalem and the Temple would become the centre of the world

- the Messiah would usher in a period of perfect peace and happiness, with God's rule of justice and mercy established for ever over all people.

These beliefs had developed over many years. At the time of Jesus, the expectation was of a Messiah who was a human leader who would come to free Israel from the Roman occupation.

According to Mark, Jesus avoided using the title 'Christ' or 'Messiah', perhaps because he did not want to be seen by the Jews as a military leader. It is clear that Jesus saw God's kingdom as ushering in a time of peace not war.

When Peter spoke out at Caesarea Philippi, 'You are the Christ' (Mark 8:27), Jesus warned his disciples to tell no one.

The next time the title was used was at Jesus' trial before the Sanhedrin, when he was asked outright by the High Priest, 'Are you the Messiah, the Son of the Blessed One?' and Jesus replied, 'I am' (Mark 14:61). By this stage, Jesus had been arrested, so there was no reason to avoid the title.

One event does demonstrate Jesus as the Messianic King, and that is his entry to Jerusalem on Palm Sunday: 'Hosanna! Blessed is he who comes in the name of the Lord!' (Mark 11:9 and Psalm 118:25–26).

What is the significance for Christians today?

Early Christians very soon started to call Jesus the Messiah because they believed that they had seen God at work in him: in his life, his death and his resurrection. Today's Christians also recognise God at work in Jesus and can identify with the hope that the Jews had as they sought the Messiah who would free them from their sufferings and restore God's kingdom. For Christians, Jesus, the Messiah, will guide them through their problems to bring them back to God.

The world has changed little as far as injustice and suffering go. Violence, poverty, disease and starvation continue to bring suffering to many in spite of the advances in medicine and technology. Christians have been in the forefront of the fight against injustice, whether you think of high-profile figures like Mother Teresa or Martin Luther King, or the many thousands who have joined campaigns like the Make Poverty History or the Jubilee Trust. It is not just Christians who have been involved in these, for many non-Christian individuals share these concerns about injustice, but Christians are commanded as followers of Christ to work for the peace and harmony of all people under God and stand against the evils in the world.

Activities

2 How does Jesus reflect the traditional Jewish ideas of a Messiah?

3 In what ways was Jesus different from these ideas?

4 How did Jesus show his claim to be the Messiah as he entered Jerusalem on Palm Sunday?

ResultsPlus
Top Tip!

Just because this topic does not focus on a specific passage in Mark's gospel does not mean that you shouldn't use quotes in your answer. Supporting your answer with details will improve your response.

For discussion

- Some Jews who convert to Christianity today call themselves Messianic Jews. Why do you think they do this?
- Why do you think it is important for Christians to have a Messiah figure today?

Summary

This lesson has looked at the meaning of the name 'Messiah' and how Jesus fitted the profile during his time on Earth. The lesson then looked at the significance of the idea of the Messiah for Christians today.

4.10 Jesus – the Son of Man

Learning outcomes

By the end of this lesson, you should be able to:

- describe the use of the title 'Son of Man' for Jesus in Mark's gospel

- give your own opinion, with a reason, about what this title shows about Jesus

- explain the significance of the title for Christians today and express your own point of view.

The Transfiguration (1519–1520) by Raphael shows Jesus with the disciples Peter, James and John during the transfiguration. Afterwards, as they came down the mountain, Jesus gave them orders not to tell anyone what they had seen until the 'Son of Man' had risen from the dead.

edexcel ::: key terms

Son of Man – A title used by Jesus of himself, probably meaning he would suffer before bringing in God's kingdom.

Why 'Son of Man'?

This was the title that Mark used, particularly when Jesus was speaking about himself. So why would he have chosen this, rather than Messiah or Son of God?

- Did Jesus use it to avoid causing trouble with the authorities perhaps? This way he would not appear to be making claims to be the Messiah, and so he would be able to carry on his mission without being misunderstood and quickly arrested.

- Alternatively, some people think that Jesus used it because it was a title for the Messiah, found in the Old Testament book of Daniel, chapter 7. In one of Daniel's visions he saw four great beasts that represented four great nations rising up to oppress the Jewish people. The 'Ancient of Days' (taken to mean God himself), sat in judgement over these nations, and gave 'one like a son of man' authority to govern and to be worshipped by the people. This son of man is taken to represent God's saints.

Jesus called himself the **Son of Man** three times in the gospel, and each time it is linked with persecution of himself or his followers:

- In the first instance, Jesus was explaining what it meant to be a disciple: 'If anyone is ashamed of me and my words in this adulterous and sinful generation, the Son of Man will be ashamed of him when he comes in his Father's glory with the holy angels' (Mark 8:38).

- In the second passage, Jesus was talking about the signs that would point to the end of the world: 'At that time men will see the Son of Man coming in clouds with great power and glory' (Mark 13:26).
- The third passage was at the trial before the High Priest. When Jesus was asked if he was the Christ: 'I am, said Jesus. And you will see the Son of Man sitting at the right hand of the Mighty One and coming on the clouds of heaven' (Mark 14:62).

Mark also used the title to show that Jesus had authority from God, an authority that meant he could do things that only God can. When Jesus heals the paralytic man, Mark states, '... the Son of Man has authority on earth to forgive sins' (Mark 2:10a) and when his disciples are challenged for eating ears of corn as they walk through the field, he says: 'So the Son of Man is Lord even of the Sabbath' (Mark 2:28).

The majority of the sayings of Jesus about the Son of Man are to do with themes of suffering, death and resurrection. As such, they would be linked with another Old Testament book, Isaiah, in which the Suffering Servant is described. Jesus saw his suffering as a punishment, not for anything that he had done wrong, but for the sins of other people. This was why he said, 'For even the Son of Man did not come to be served, but to serve, and to give his life as a ransom for many' (Mark 10:45).

> 'This will happen when the Lord Jesus is revealed from heaven in blazing fire with his powerful angels. He will punish those who do not know God and do not obey the gospel of our Lord Jesus.'
> (2 Thessalonians 1:7–9)

The prospect of judgement and hell is not appealing, and some hold the idea that everyone will end up with God in heaven. God's love is so great that he will not turn away anyone, no matter what they have done. Others are concerned that the opposite view will prevail, and that God will condemn people at the time of judgement. In other words, their discipleship will be judged.

The suffering theme for the Son of Man remains as relevant today as ever, for Christians believe that Jesus came to save people from the power of sin and to call them back to God. Jesus' first words in the gospel were: 'The time has come.... The kingdom of God is near. Repent and believe the good news!' (Mark 1:15). This summarised his message and everything that followed was directed toward this purpose, even when Jesus was rejected and killed. His sacrifice did not end the story, for the resurrection followed.

Those who accept that Jesus died and rose again to enable them to be united with God believe that they will be saved from the power of evil, called sin.

Activities

1 In seven other places Mark writes of this theme. To complete the picture of Jesus, the Son of Man who must suffer, look up the following verses from Mark and note down what is predicted: 8:31, 9:9, 9:12, 9:31, 10:33–34, 14:21, 14:41–42.

2 **Hot-seat activity – interview with Mark.** Choose someone to put themselves in Mark's shoes. Ask Mark why he decided to called Jesus the Son of Man.

Activities

3 Explain why you think Jesus used the title 'Son of Man' more than any other title?

4 What are the main themes of the idea of the Son of Man?

5 What is the significance of the title to Christians today?

What does the title mean to Christians today?

People do not use this title very often when talking about Jesus, but it is still important for the message it conveys: that Jesus will return to judge humanity.

Summary

Mark used the title 'Son of Man' to describe Jesus several times. It is not often used today but is still important.

4.11 Jesus – the Son of God

> **Learning outcomes**
>
> By the end of this lesson, you should be able to:
>
> - describe the use of the title 'Son of God' in Mark's gospel
> - give your own opinion, with a reason, about what this title shows about Jesus
> - explain why reading the gospel may lead some people to believe that Jesus was the Son of God.

Mark's use of the title 'Son of God'

Right at the start of his gospel, Mark sets out his belief in who Jesus is – the Messiah and the Son of God:

> 'The beginning of the gospel about Jesus Christ, the Son of God.' (Mark 1:1)

In many ways these are the most popular titles given to Jesus today, although Mark restricted their use in his gospel. The title 'Son of God' appears only at the opening of Jesus' ministry and then again at his crucifixion, when the centurion says, 'Truly this man was a son of God' (Mark 15:39). As Mark makes his own statement of faith at the beginning of the gospel, he points back to the opening of Genesis, the first book in the Bible, where it says, 'In the beginning God created the heavens and the earth' (Genesis 1:1), and in doing so he declares that Jesus is the Son of God, a divine person.

Why readers of Mark's gospel might come to believe that Jesus was the Son of God

As well as these two verses, there are a number of passages in Mark's gospel that could lead readers to believe that Jesus was the Son of God.

There are two occasions where people heard the voice of God the Father speaking from heaven to identify Jesus as his son. Look back to Jesus' baptism in Mark 1:11 (page 94) and then his transfiguration in Mark 9:7 (page 98).

These words would also remind Mark's readers of parts of the Old Testament:

> 'He said to me, You are my Son; today I have become your Father.' (Psalm 2:7b)

The prophet Hosea refers to the nation of Israel's God being their Father who has a son:

> 'When Israel was a child, I loved him, and out of Egypt I called my son.' (Hosea 11:1)

Isaiah also has echoes of God the Father's words:

> 'Here is my servant, whom I uphold, my chosen one in whom I delight; I will put my Spirit on him and he will bring justice to the nations.' (Isaiah 42:1)

In doing this, Mark links Jesus to the Jewish idea of the Son of God.

In one place Jesus himself claimed to be the Son of God. At the trial before the High Priest when he was asked, 'Are you the Christ, the Son of the Blessed One?' Jesus replied, 'I am. And you will see the Son of Man sitting at the right hand of the Mighty One and coming on the clouds of heaven' (Mark 14:61b, 62). This was blasphemy to the Jewish authorities, but Christians believe that Jesus was speaking the truth.

One further story points to Jesus being the Son of God. In the parable of the tenants (see pages 14–15) Jesus says, 'He had one left to send, a son, whom he loved. He sent him last of all, saying, "They will respect my son."' (Mark 12:6). The parable speaks of God's plan of salvation for humankind.

For discussion

Which example from Mark's gospel would most convince a reader that Jesus was the Son of God?

What does 'Son of God' mean for the Church?

The Christian Church used these titles from the beginning when talking about Jesus. Early Christians believed that God was at work in Jesus, in his life, his death and resurrection. They believed that Jesus was 'the radiance of God's glory and the exact representation of his being, sustaining all things by his powerful word' (Hebrews 1:3a).

As the Church expanded beyond Jerusalem, taking in more Gentiles, the Greek and Roman influence increased and with it the use of the title 'Son of God'. This was because, for them, the title signified a divine nature.

Christians believe that there is only one God. There are three persons – Father, Son and Holy Spirit – but they are not divided, so that there is just one God. This is the doctrine of the Trinity.

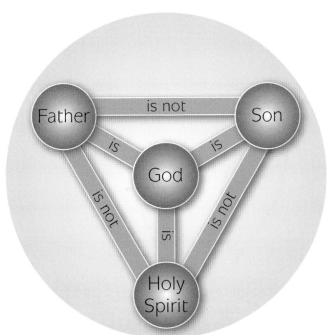

The Trinity shield illustrates the 'mystery' of the Trinity.

Many people have difficulty picturing what God is like as he is not a human being. Calling God 'Father' or 'Son' gives an image only, for God the Father is seen as perfect – all-knowing, all-powerful and everywhere, unlike a human father. Christians believe that Jesus showed people what God was like: he was a human being from a humble, ordinary background and, as such, someone humans could understand – but at the same time he also mirrored the perfect qualities associated with God.

Activities

1   In what ways do you think it is helpful for Christians to remember Jesus was a real human being like themselves?

2   Go to www.pearsonschoolsandfecolleges. co.uk/hotlinks (express code 4271P) and click on the appropriate link to find out more about the Trinity and what Christians understand about this doctrine. Draw a picture of one of the symbols used to represent the Trinity.

3   What did it mean to the early Christians to remember Jesus as the Christ, the Son of God?

4   How different is the understanding of Christians today when they believe that Jesus is the Son of God?

Summary

There are many parts of Mark's gospel that could lead people to believe that Jesus was the Son of God. Mark uses the title to describe Jesus twice, plus on two other occasions, Jesus' baptism and transfiguration. Mark writes of a voice from heaven – God the Father's – identifying Jesus as his dearly loved son. 'Son of God' is a very important title of Jesus for Christians today.

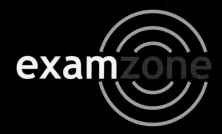

examzone

KnowZone
The identity of Jesus

Quick quiz

1 What title does Mark start with in the opening verse?

2 Who baptised Jesus at the beginning of Mark's gospel?

3 Who first identifies Jesus as the 'Messiah' according to Mark's gospel?

4 What is meant by 'transfiguration'?

5 What are the two different types of baptism that are practised by Christians today?

6 What is meant by the term 'nature miracle'?

7 Give two examples of nature miracles in Mark's gospel.

8 What is meant by the term 'healing miracle'?

9 Give two examples of healing miracles in Mark's gospel.

10 What three titles does Mark use when he describes Jesus?

Find out more

The following books are good places to find out more:

- *Mark's gospel – An Interpretation for Today* by Robin Cooper (Hodder, ISBN 0-340-43029-X)

- *Mark: A Gospel for Today* 3rd ed by Simon and Christopher Danes (St Mark's Press, ISBN 9-781-9070-6200-1)

- *Revise GCSE Religious Studies* (Letts, ISBN-13 9-781-8431-5515-7)

- You can also find out more in the Christianity section of the BBC's Religion website. Go to www.pearsonschoolsandfecolleges.co.uk/hotlinks (express code 4271P) and click on the appropriate link.

Student tips

I found it really useful to make revision cards of the key words for this section. I could then study them myself and give them to other people to test me! This really helped in answering the first question on the exam, where you have to define key words, but it also meant that I could use the key words in my other answers too.

Plenary activity

Design an ideas map of the different topics in this section on the identity of Jesus. The one here has been started to give you some help.

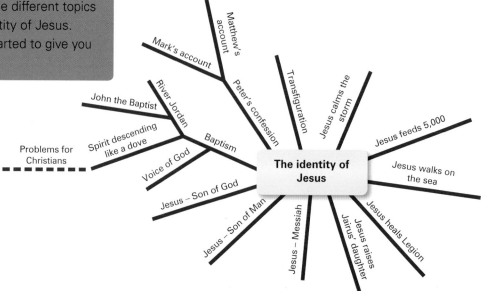

Self-evaluation checklist

How well have you understood the topics in this section? In the first column of the table below use the following code to rate your understanding:

Green – I understand this fully.

Orange – I am confident I can answer most questions on this.

Red – I need to do a lot more work on this topic.

In the second and third columns you need to think about:

● whether you have an opinion on this topic and could give reasons for that opinion if asked

● whether you can give the opinion of someone who disagrees with you and give reasons for this alternative opinion.

Content covered	My understanding is red/orange/green	Can I give my opinion?	Can I give an alternative opinion?
● What the baptism shows about Jesus for Mark			
● Why this causes problems for some Christians today			
● What Peter's confession at Caesarea Philippi shows about Jesus in Mark's gospel			
● Why Matthew's record is more important for Roman Catholic Christians today			
● What the transfiguration shows about Jesus for Mark			
● Why the transfiguration causes problems for some Christians today			
● What the calming of the storm shows about Jesus for Mark			
● Why the calming of the storm causes problems for some Christians today			
● What the feeding of the five thousand shows about Jesus for Mark			
● Why the feeding of the five thousand causes problems for some Christians today			
● What the walking on the sea shows about Jesus for Mark			
● Why the walking on the sea causes problems for some Christians today			
● What the healing of Legion shows about Jesus for Mark			
● Why the healing of Legion causes problems for some Christians today			
● What the raising of Jairus' daughter shows about Jesus for Mark			
● Why the raising of Jairus' daughter causes problems for some Christians today			
● What the title 'Messiah' shows about Jesus and its significance for Christians today			
● What the title 'Son of Man' shows about Jesus and its significance for Christians today			
● Why reading Mark's gospel leads some people to believe that Jesus was the Son of God			

examzone

KnowZone
The identity of Jesus

Introduction

In the exam you will see a choice of two questions on this section. Each question will include four tasks that test your knowledge, understanding and evaluation of the material covered. A 2-mark question will ask you to define a term; a 4-mark question will ask you to give your opinion on a point of view; an 8-mark question will ask you to explain a particular belief or idea; a 6-mark question will ask for your opinion on a point of view and ask you to consider an alternative point of view.

Here you need to give a short accurate definition. You do not need to write more than one clear sentence.

The important words in the question are 'explain why', so you must make sure that this is what you focus on in your answer. This is worth 8 marks, so you must be prepared to spend some time answering it. You will also be assessed on your use of language in this question.

As before, give reasons you have learned in class. You must show you understand why people have these other views, even if you don't agree with them.

Mini exam paper

(a) Who was **Jairus**? (2 marks)

(b) Do you think Jesus could walk on water?

Give **two** reasons for your point of view. (4 marks)

(c) Explain why the transfiguration causes problems for some Christians today. (8 marks)

(d) 'If Jesus was baptised he must have been sinful.'

In your answer you should refer to Mark's gospel and Christianity.

(i) Do you agree? Give reasons for your opinion. (3 marks)

(ii) Give reasons why some people may disagree with you. (3 marks)

You must give your opinion but make sure you do give two clear and properly thought-out reasons. These can be ones you have learned in class.

In your answer you should state whether you agree or disagree with the statement, and you need to support your opinion with reasons.

Mark scheme

(a) You can earn **2 marks** for a correct answer, and **1 mark** for a partially correct answer.

(b) To earn up to the full **4 marks** you need to give two reasons and develop them. Two brief reasons or only one developed reason will earn **2 marks**.

(c) You can earn **7–8 marks** by giving up to four reasons, but the fewer reasons you give, the more you must develop them. Because you are being assessed on use of language, you also need to take care to express your understanding in a clear style of English and make some use of specialist vocabulary.

(d) To go beyond **3 marks** for the whole of this question you must refer to Christianity and Mark's gospel. The marks you are able to develop your reasons, the more marks you will earn. Three simple reasons can earn you the same mark as one fully developed reason.

Results Plus
Build Better Answers

(c) Explain why the transfiguration causes problems for some Christians today. (8 marks)

Student answer	Comments	Improved student answer
The transfiguration causes problems for some Christians today because they would not expect the disciples to run away when he was arrested. If the disciples had understood who he was at the transfiguration, they would surely have trusted him to look after them at the arrest. Also, how were the disciples able to recognise the people who were with Jesus? Christians today may not understand the importance of Moses and Elijah.	The first paragraph gives a developed reason, and the second gives a brief reason. This would gain 6 marks. The answer is in a clear style of English and uses some specialist vocabulary. To improve the answer, the student would need to develop the second paragraph with more explanation, or bring in another reason for the problems.	The transfiguration causes problems for some Christians today because they would not expect the disciples to run away when he was arrested. If the disciples had understood who he was at the transfiguration, they would surely have trusted him to look after them at the arrest. Also, how were the disciples able to recognise the people who were with Jesus? Christians today may not understand the importance of Moses and Elijah. Those Christians who had not studied the Old Testament may not appreciate the significance of the two characters. Moses was the Lawgiver, who led the Children of Israel out of slavery in Egypt. Elijah was one of the prophets in the Old Testament, one who had raised people from the dead and was commonly expected to appear before the arrival of the Messiah.

Welcome to examzone

Revising for your exams can be a daunting prospect. In this part of the book we'll take you through the process of revising for your exams, step by step, to help you prepare as well as you can

Zone In!

Have you ever become so absorbed in a task that suddenly it feels entirely natural and easy to perform? This is a feeling familiar to many athletes and performers. They work hard to recreate it in competition in order to do their very best. It's a feeling of being 'in the zone', and if you can achieve that same feeling in an examination, the chances are you'll perform brilliantly.

The good news is that you can get 'in the zone' by taking some simple steps in advance of the exam. Below are some points to consider.

UNDERSTAND IT

Make sure you understand the exam process and what revision you need to do. This will give you confidence and also help you to get things into proportion.

FRIENDS AND FAMILY

Make sure that your friends and family know when you want to revise. Even share your revision plan with them. Learn to control your times with them, so you don't get distracted. This means you can have better quality time with them when you aren't revising, because you aren't worrying about what you ought to be doing.

DEAL WITH DISTRACTIONS

Think about the issues in your life that may interfere with revision. Write them all down. Then think about how you can deal with each so they don't affect your revision.

COMPARTMENTALISE

You might not be able to deal with all the issues that can distract you. For example, you may be worried about a friend who is ill, or just be afraid of the exam. In this case, there is still a useful technique you can use. Put all of these worries into an imagined box in your mind at the start of your revision (or in the exam) and mentally lock it. Only open it again at the end of your revision session (or exam).

DIET AND EXERCISE

Make sure you eat sensibly and exercise as well! If your body is not in the right state, how can your mind be? A substantial breakfast will set you up for the day, and a light evening meal will keep your energy levels high.

BUILD CONFIDENCE

Use your revision time not only to revise content, but also to build your confidence in readiness for tackling the examination. For example, try tackling a short sequence of easy tasks in record time.

 More on the CD

The key to success in exams and revision often lies in good planning. Knowing **what** you need to do and **when** you need to do it is your best path to a stress-free experience. Here are some tips for creating a great personal revision plan.

First of all, *know your strengths and weaknesses.*

Go through each topic making a list of how well you think you know the topic. Use your mock examination results and/or any other test results that are available as a check on your self-assessment. This will help you to plan your personal revision effectively, putting extra time into your weaker areas.

Next, *create your plan!*

Remember to make time for considering how topics interrelate.

For example, in PE you will be expected to know not just about the various muscles, but how these relate to various body types.

The specification quite clearly states when you are expected to be able to link one topic to another so plan this into your revision sessions. You will be tested on this in the exam.

Finally, *follow the plan!*

You can use the revision sections in the following pages to kick-start your revision.

MAY

SUNDAY	MONDAY	TUES
	30	1
7	8	
13		
20		22
27	28	

Be realistic about how much time you can devote to your revision, but also make sure you put in enough time. Give yourself regular breaks or different activities to give your life some variance. Revision need not be a prison sentence!

Find out your exam dates. Go to the Edexcel website **www.edexcel.com** to find all final exam dates, and check with your teacher.

iew Secti
complete t
ractice ex
question

Chunk your revision in each subject down into smaller sections. This will make it more manageable and less daunting.

Draw up a list of all the dates from the start of your revision right through to your exams.

Review Sectio
Complete three
practice exam

Review Sectio
Try the Keywor
Quiz again

Make sure you allow time for assessing your progress against your initial self-assessment. Measuring progress will allow you to see and be encouraged by your improvement. These little victories will build your confidence.

EXAM DAY!

For all sections of the examination, you need to show the examiner that you understand the nature of Mark's gospel and its effects on the lives of Christians today (AO1). You also need to be able give your own point of view and an alternative point of view, explaining the reasons why you, and others, may think like this (AO2). What is important is the reasons that you give for your opinion so make sure that you focus on these.

Exam question tips for all sections

Questions of type (a)
Your answers should give the glossary definitions of the key words! Make sure you know them!

Questions of type (b)
These questions are seeking your opinion but you must go beyond describing what you think. Your answer must be supported by TWO reasons and you need to explain how these reasons support your opinion.

Questions of type (c)
Questions here are asking you either:

To explain why ..., which demands that you use the word because ... in your answer.

Or:

To explain how ..., which means that you should say how two things are connected. Remember you have to explain. It is not enough just to give a description.

Questions of type (d)
Answers must be a response to the statement, so make sure that this is what you write.

Give reasons for agreeing or not agreeing with the statement. If you agree, then say so and give the opposite opinion, with reasons. You must refer directly to Mark's gospel and/or how other Christians might respond so make sure you do this either in part (i) or part (ii) or both!

Revision

Look back at the KnowZones at the end of each section (pages 26–29, 56–59, 88–91, 116–119). Spend some time reading through each self-evaluation chart and think about which are your stronger and weaker areas, so that you can focus on those areas you are less confident about.

You might like to try the quick quizzes or the plenary activities. If you have already completed the plenary activities, then find the ideas maps you created and use this to refresh your memory.

When you are ready for some exam practice, read through the questions, advice and answers on pages 28–29, 58–59, 90–91 and 118–119. Then you could have a go at the exam questions on the next page.

Practice Exam Questions

Section 1

(a) Who was **Levi**? *(2 marks)*

(b) Do you think serving God is more important than loving your family?

Give **two** reasons for your point of view. *(4 marks)*

(c) Explain why Mark's account of the parable of the sower causes problems for Christians today. *(8 marks)*

(d) 'The disciples of Jesus show people how to live today.'

In your answer you should refer to Christianity.

  (i) Do you agree? Give reasons for your opinion. *(3 marks)*

  (ii) Give reasons why some people may disagree with you. *(3 marks)*

Practice Exam Questions

Section 2

(a) What is **corban**? *(2marks)*

(b) Do you think Christians today should obey the Sabbath laws?

Give **two** reasons for your point of view. *(4 marks)*

(c) Explain why Jesus' disagreements with the Pharisees about the meaning of the Law are significant for current arguments about social cohesion. *(8 marks)*

(d) 'The woman at Bethany was right to anoint Jesus.'

In your answer you should refer to Mark's Gospel and Christianity.

  (i) Do you agree? Give reasons for your opinion. *(3 marks)*

  (ii) Give reasons why some people may disagree with you. *(3 marks)*

Practice Exam Questions

Section 3

(a) What is **Golgatha**? *(2 marks)*

(b) Do you think Judas was evil?

Give **two** reasons for your point of view. *(4 marks)*

(c) Explain why the prayers of Jesus in Gethsemane cause problems for some Christians today. *(8 marks)*

(d) 'The resurrection could not have happened.'

In your answer you should refer to Mark's gospel and Christianity.

  (i) Do you agree? Give reasons for your opinion. *(3 marks)*

  (ii) Give reasons why some people may disagree with you. *(3 marks)*

Practice Exam Questions

Section 4

(a) What is the **transfiguration**? *(2 marks)*

(b) Do you think Jesus was the Son of God?

Give **two** reasons for your point of view. *(4 marks)*

(c) Explain why Matthew's account of Peter's confession is more important for Roman Catholic Christians than Mark's. *(8 marks)*

(d) 'No one could feed five thousand people with five loaves and two fish.'

In your answer you should refer to Mark's gospel and Christianity.

  (i) Do you agree? Give reasons for your opinion. *(3 marks)*

  (ii) Give reasons why some people may disagree with you. *(3 marks)*

If you are sitting your exams from 2014 onwards, you will be sitting all the exams together at the end of the course. Make sure you know in which order you are sitting the exams and prepare for each accordingly. Check with your teacher if you are not sure. The exams are likely to be about a week apart, so make sure you allow plenty of revision time for each.

As you get close to completing your revision, the Big Day will be getting nearer and nearer. Many students find this the most stressful time and tend to go into panic mode, either working long hours without really giving their brains a chance to absorb information. or giving up and staring blankly at the wall.

Panicking simply makes your brain seize up and you find that information and thoughts simply cannot flow naturally. You become distracted and anxious, and things seem worse than they are. Many students build the exams up into more than they are. Remember: the exams are not trying to catch you out! If you have studied the course, there will be no surprises on the exam paper!

Student tip

I know how silly it is to panic, especially if you've done the work and know your stuff. I was asked by a teacher to produce a report on a project I'd done, and I panicked so much I spent the whole afternoon crying and worrying. I asked other people for help, but they were panicking too. In the end, I calmed down and looked at the task again. It turned out to be quite straightforward. I got my report finished first and it was the best of them all!

In the exam you don't have much time, so you can't waste it by panicking. The best way to control panic is simply to do what you have to do. Think carefully for a few minutes, then start writing and as you do, the panic will drain away.

Don't panic

You will have one and a half hours for this exam paper and in that time you have to answer **four** questions, one on each of the four sections you have studied: Discipleship, Conflict and argument, Death and resurrection and The identity of Jesus.

In each section, you can make a choice from two questions.

Each question will be made up of four different parts:

- a 2-mark question will ask you to define a term
- a 4-mark question will ask your opinion on a point of view
- an 8-mark question will ask you to explain a particular belief or idea
- a 6-mark question will ask for your opinion on a point of view and ask you to consider an alternative point of view.

Effectively you shouldn't spend more than 22.5 minutes on each section (that's 90 minutes divided by 4):

- the 8-mark question deserves the most attention, so that's around 9 minutes
- the 2-mark question should take you 1.5 minutes, then
- 5 minutes for the 4-mark question, and
- the remaining 7 minutes for the 6-mark question.

Obviously you can give or take a minute here or there, and your teacher may guide you differently, but as long as you don't go over 22.5 minutes altogether and the length of each of your answers is appropriate for the number of marks available, then you'll be on the right lines.

Meet the exam paper

This diagram shows the front cover of the exam paper. These instructions, information and advice will always appear on the front of the paper. It is worth reading it carefully now. Check you understand it. Now is a good opportunity to ask your teacher about anything you are not sure of here.

Print your surname here, and your other names afterwards to ensure that the exam board awards the marks to the right candidate.

Here you fill in the school's exam number.

Ensure that you understand exactly how long the examination will last, and plan your time accordingly.

Note that the quality of your written communication will also be marked. Take particular care to present your thoughts and work at the highest standard you can, for maximum marks.

Here you fill in your personal exam number. Take care when writing it down because the number is important to the exam board when writing your score.

In this box, the examiner will write the total marks you have achieved in the exam paper.

Make sure that you understand exactly which questions from which sections you should attempt.

Don't feel that you have to fill the answer space provided. Everybody's handwriting varies, so a long answer from one person may take up the same space as a short answer from someone else.

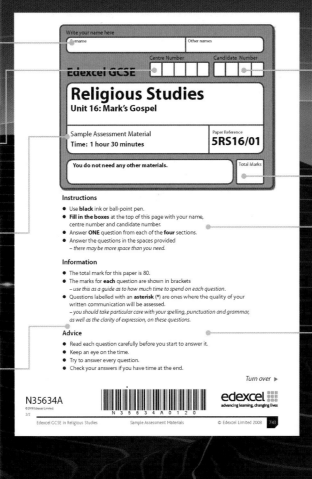

Write your name here
Surname | Other names

Centre Number | Candidate Number

Edexcel GCSE

Religious Studies
Unit 16: Mark's Gospel

Sample Assessment Material
Time: 1 hour 30 minutes

Paper Reference
5RS16/01

You do not need any other materials. | Total Marks

Instructions

- Use **black** ink or ball-point pen.
- **Fill in the boxes** at the top of this page with your name, centre number and candidate number.
- Answer **ONE** question from each of the **four** sections.
- Answer the questions in the spaces provided
  – there may be more space than you need.

Information

- The total mark for this paper is 80.
- The marks for **each** question are shown in brackets
  – use this as a guide as to how much time to spend on each question.
- Questions labelled with an **asterisk** (*) are ones where the quality of your written communication will be assessed.
  – you should take particular care with your spelling, punctuation and grammar, as well as the clarity of expression, on these questions.

Advice

- Read each question carefully before you start to answer it.
- Keep an eye on the time.
- Try to answer every question.
- Check your answers if you have time at the end.

Turn over ▶

N35634A
©2008 Edexcel Limited.
2/2

Edexcel GCSE in Religious Studies | Sample Assessment Materials | © Edexcel Limited 2008 | 7/3

edexcel
advancing learning, changing lives

Practical tips on the exam paper

- You must use a black pen. Your paper is scanned into a computer for marking. If you write in any other colour, you risk your work not being seen clearly.

- You must choose your question carefully. It is a good idea to cross out the one you are not going to do – to avoid changing a questions half-way through your answer. This is a very common mistake and would lose you marks!

- Mark with an x at the top of the page which question you have chosen.

- Do not write outside the guidelines – your answer may get cut off by the scanning process.

- Do not use extra sheets and attach them unless it is absolutely necessary. If you need more space – for example, for a (b) question – continue into the (c) space and when you change question write your own (c). Do the same for (c) into (d). If you then run out, put an arrow and write at the end of the exam booklet.

This section provides answers to the most common questions students have about what happens after they complete their exams. For more information, visit www.pearsonschoolsandfecolleges.co.uk/hotlinks (express code 4271P) and click on examzone.

About your grades

Whether you've done better than, worse than, or just as you expected, your grades are the final measure of your performance on your course and in the exams. On this page we explain some of the information that appears on your results slip and tell you what to do if you think something is wrong. We answer the most popular questions about grades and look at some of the options facing you.

When will my results be published?

Results for GCSE summer examinations are issued on the third Thursday in August. January exam results are issued in March and March exam results issued in April.

If you are sitting your exams from 2014 onwards, there will no longer be January sittings: you will sit all of your exams in June.

Can I get my results online?

Visit the resultsplus direct website. Go to www.pearsonschoolsandfecolleges. co.uk/hotlinks (express code 4271P) and click on the appropriate link, where you will find detailed student results information including the 'Edexcel Gradeometer' which demonstrates how close you were to the nearest grade boundary.

I haven't done as well as I expected. What can I do now?

First of all, talk to your subject teacher. After all the teaching that you have had, tests and internal examinations, he/she is the person who best knows what grade you are capable of achieving. Take your results slip to your subject teacher, and go through the information on it in detail. If you both think there is something wrong with the result, the school or college can apply to see your completed examination paper and then, if necessary, ask for a re-mark immediately. Bear in mind that he original mark can be confirmed or lowered, as well as raised, as a result of a re-mark.

How do my grades compare with those of everybody else who sat this exam?

You can compare your results with those of others in the UK who have completed the same examination using the information on the Edexcel website. Go to www.pearsonschoolsandfecolleges.co.uk/hotlinks (express code 4271P) and click on the appropriate link.

What happens if I was ill over the period of my examinations?

If you become ill before or during the examination period you are eligible for special consideration. This also applies if you have been affected by an accident, bereavement or serious disturbance during an examination.

If my school has requested special consideration for me, is this shown on my Statement of Results?

If your school has requested special consideration for you, it is not shown on your results slip, but it will be shown on a subject mark report that is sent to your school or college. If you want to know whether special consideration was requested for you, you should ask your Examinations Officer.

Can I have a re-mark of my examination paper?

Yes, this is possible, but remember that only your school or college can apply for a re-mark, not you or your parents/carers. First of all, you should consider carefully whether or not to ask your school or college to make a request for a re-mark. It is worth knowing that very few re-marks result in a change to a grade – not because Edexcel is embarrassed that a change of marks has been made, but simply because a re-mark request has shown that the original marking was accurate. Check the closing date for re-marking requests with your Examinations Officer.

When I asked for a re-mark of my paper, my subject grade went down. What can I do?

There is no guarantee that your grades will go up if your papers are re-marked. They can also go down or stay the same. After a re-mark, the only way to improve your grade is to take the examination again. Your school or college Examinations Officer can tell you when you can do that.

Can I re-sit this unit?

If you are sitting your exams before 2014, you may re-sit a unit once prior to claiming certification for the qualification. The highest score obtained on either the first attempt or the re-sit counts towards your final grade.

If you are sitting your exams from 2014 onwards, you will not be able to re-sit any of the exams.

For much more information, go to www.pearsonschoolsandfecolleges.co.uk/hotlinks (express code 4271P) and click on examzone.

Glossary

This is an extended glossary containing definitions that will help you in your studies. Edexcel key terms are not included as all of these are defined in the lessons themselves.

Acts of the Apostles – The fifth book of the New Testament, commonly referred to as Acts. It outlines the history of the Twelve Apostles after the crucifixion. The author is traditionally identified as Luke.

Anglican churches – Group of **Protestant** churches whose mother church is the **Church of England**.

anti-Semitism – Prejudice against or hostility towards the Jewish people.

anointing – **Sacrament** in which perfumed oil, or water, is poured or smeared onto the skin to symbolise the healing or cleansing power of God. Used in baptism. 'Messiah' is the Hebrew word for 'anointed one' and 'Christ' is the Greek word.

apostolic – The belief that the Church is founded on the apostles who were appointed by Jesus.

atonement – Reconciliation between God and humanity through Jesus' sacrifice on the cross.

Baptist churches – Group of **Nonconformist** churches committed to believers' baptism and the idea that all believers are priests.

Barabbas – Jewish criminal who was freed by Pontius Pilate, who offered to free Jesus instead.

Caesarea Philippi – Ancient Roman city near which Peter made his confession of Jesus as the Messiah.

Church of England – **Protestant** church formed by Henry VIII, which is the mother church of the **Anglican Communion**.

consubstantiation – Belief that Jesus is really present in the bread and wine offered in the **Eucharist**, but that there is no real change in the bread or wine. The **Lutheran Church** and some members of the **Church of England** hold to this view.

demons – Evil spirits. Stories of possession by evil spirits appear in many gospel stories. Many people nowadays discount this as superstition, and believe that when the gospels talk of possession by demons they are describing mental illness. Others remain convinced of the reality of demons and spirits.

Eastern Orthodox Church – That part of the **apostolic** Christian Church found in Eastern Europe and Russia: it is not part of the **Roman Catholic Church**.

Eucharist – **Sacrament** of blessing and giving bread and wine as a memorial of the Last Supper and of Christ's **atonement** on the cross.

Gentiles – Jewish name for non-Jewish people: Christians believe Jesus was Messiah for both Jews and Gentiles.

heaven – A place of paradise where God rules.

hell – A place of horrors where Satan rules.

kosher – Anything that conforms to the Jewish Law; most often used for food.

leper – Someone who suffers from leprosy, a dangerous, contagious and unsightly skin disease.

Lutheran Church – A major Protestant church that receives its name from the 16th-century German reformer Martin Luther.

Memorialism – Belief that the bread and wine offered in the **Eucharist** are no more than symbols, intended to remind believers of Jesus' death and resurrection. Most **Nonconformist** Churches hold to this view.

Methodist Church – **Protestant** church which came into existence through the work of John Wesley in the 18th century.

Nonconformist churches – **Protestant churches** separated from their mother church, the **Church of England**.

Original Sin – The sin that mankind is born with, resulting from the Fall of Adam and Eve in the Garden of Eden.

parable – A story used to illustrate a moral or spiritual lesson. Jesus told many parables.

Paul – Pharisee and persecutor of Christians who was converted to Christianity on the road to Damascus, after which he became a Christian missionary. Paul is responsible for much of the teaching of the early Church: thirteen letters in the New Testament are attributed to Paul.

patriarch – Abraham, his son Isaac and his grandson Jacob; according to the Old Testament the three male founders of the Jewish people.

Peter – One of Jesus' disciples. 'Peter' in Greek is Petros, so when Jesus said 'On this rock I will build my church', he meant that the Church would be built from Peter's leadership. He was the first Pope of the **Roman Catholic Church**.

Pope – The Bishop of Rome and the head of the **Roman Catholic Church**.

Protestant churches – That part of the Christian Church that became distinct from the Roman Catholic and other churches, when their members 'protested' against the authority of the **Roman Catholic Church**. As a general rule, Protestantism rejects the doctrine of **apostolic** succession.

Receptionism – Belief that Jesus is really present in the bread and the wine offered at the moment they are consumed in a spiritual way in the **Eucharist**. Most of the **Church of England** holds to this view.

resurrection – Belief that there is bodily life after death. Christians believe Jesus was resurrected three days after the crucifixion, on Easter Sunday.

Roman Catholic Church – That part of the **apostolic** Christian Church led by the **Pope**; believes that **Peter** was the first Pope.

Second Coming – The belief that Jesus will return to earth in the future.

transubstantiation – **Roman Catholic** belief that the bread and wine offered in the **Eucharist** become the actual body and blood of Jesus.

Trinity – The belief that God is three in one; the Father, the Son and the Holy Spirit.

Western Wall – The Western (or Wailing) Wall is all that remains of the Temple today and is a holy site for Jews.

Zealots – Group of people whose aim was to expel the Roman Empire from Jewish lands.

Index

In the following index, Edexcel key terms are given in **bold** and the first page number, also in bold, will lead you to the definition. For further definitions of unfamiliar words, see also the Glossary on pages 128–129.